Praise fo
2 Second L

D0252016

"This is the story of Paul Akers' personal quest with his agonizing call to adventure, exploring ne.. ~~possibilities (in Japan, at FastCap~~ and in his life), his path of mistakes and revelations, and eventually achieving the prize - the truth about the heart and soul of Lean. Through photos of Paul's Lean journey, we come to know the person, the process of being Lean, and the principles that change everything. Paul demonstrates the same spirit of adventure that I imagine the engineers at Ford™ and Toyota™ must have felt those many years ago – a spirit so often lost in modern Lean.

2 Second Lean is a tangible embodiment of the principles. It's fast, effective and delivers tons of value. No consultant-speak or keeper-of-the-faith orthodoxy here, but a deeper, almost spiritual, grasp of being Lean.

This remarkable book stands out among the plethora of Lean books. If you're new to Lean, get this book! If you're a Lean expert, get this book! Either way, it won't disappoint."

~Randall Benson - Lean Consultant and author of *The Quest Effect*

"This is awesome. Love all the photos. Love the home applications. If all Lean 'gurus' practiced what they preached. ....hmmmm...."

~Holly Duckworth, Ph.D. - Kaiser Aluminum Vice President of Continuous Improvement

"I met Paul Akers of FastCap more than one year ago. Paul personally visited the City of Ferndale and spent time with employees teaching the concepts of "Lean."

We have continued Paul's teaching and embrace and use the Lean principles he writes so eloquently about in *2 Second Lean* on a daily basis. Each Friday morning we have our Lean roundtable. Lean is such an important part of what government should be and do. The public many times has a distorted opinion of government employees. Our city employees have embraced the concept of constantly seeking out improvements and efficiencies to their job duties.

I'm most impressed with how all employees interact and share ideas for improvement. This has brought more of a team atmosphere than has been exhibited in the past. Every person, from the new employee to the long-time veteran, should feel they have value and their ideas can make a difference.

Every city should explore what LEAN can do!"

~Gary S. Jensen - Mayor, City of Ferndale, Washington

"Learn how to operate with the maximum efficiency while creating a productive and positive environment in all that you do. The excellent examples and analysis in this book are a great primer for anyone seeking successful growth."
~Dr. Nido Qubein - President, High Point University and Chairman, Great Harvest Bread Co.

"Paul Akers has a passion for Lean that is totally infectious. FastCap continues on their Lean journey to continuously improve. Their approach to engaging employees for their ideas is World Class and it shows with everything Paul and his team do."
~Harry W. Kenworthy - Principal & Manager at Lean Government Center

"A great book from Paul Akers - my Lean 'brother from another mother.' Paul shows you that Lean is simple stuff that is fun and really works! *2 Second Lean* is a Lean Leadership and Culture story that will help you DO good, FEEL good, and RAISE THE TIDE for your whole organization. "
~Karl Wadensten - President Vibco Vibrators and Radio Talk Show Host *Lean Nation* on AM790 and 790Business.com

"This powerful book takes you into the dynamic world of FastCap without the airfare. You'll discover the powerful improvement community that Paul Akers' simplicity, humility and enthusiasm created. As Paul notes - we have it backwards. And when we turn our thinking around, we'll do things we never imagined possible. That's why it heartens me to know that Paul teaches his continuous improvement principles to government. Despite his claim that *2 Second Lean* is not for MBAs or those who love theory, I recommend improvement experts everywhere read it for a dash of simplicity. This book brings Lean to life. "
~Meryl Runion, CSP, author of PowerPhrases and nine other books on collaborative communication

"Everybody tells you how to implement Lean... but Paul reveals the values that make Lean grow from within your people. In my opinion, that is the significant contribution this book makes to the broader base of knowledge. Well done."
~Tony Oliver - Denver, Colorado

"Finally! A gloriously interactive book that makes learning about Lean accessible, easy to digest, and FUN! QR Code links to videos and thought-provoking reflection exercises engage you in an awesome reading experience..."
~Linda Kleineberg - CMO at VIBCO Vibrators

"*2 Second Lean* is GREAT! Paul Akers is an innovator, who totally gets empowerment, culture building, and customer service. You might expect just a well written book that helps you to get Lean quick... well it does that, but the structure of the book itself demonstrates innovation, creativity, and customer/reader focus. You will love it. Today's leaders are innovative, passionate, optimists. With Paul you get all three on steroids."

~Dr. Charles Schwahn,
Author of best seller Total Leaders 2.0

"Bright, fun, and smart, *2 Second Lean* is Paul Akers' recipe for getting continuous improvement going and growing – homespun and proofed on the floor of his own company, FastCap. This is the voice and spirit of an authentic American entrepreneur, showing us Lean can be applied anywhere and everywhere – and is always spelled P-E-O-P-L-E. Buckle your seat belt. You're in for a fast, powerful, and inspiring read... made even more so, thanks to the QR Code video links."

~Gwendolyn Galsworth, author of Visual Workplace/
Visual Thinking and Work That Makes Sense

"Paul Akers answers the question 'why' in his book – *2 Second Lean*. Why Lean? Paul gives the reader compelling reasons to embark on the Lean journey. I highly recommend *2 Second Lean* to anyone looking for answers to make their company or organization more efficient and more profitable.

As County Executive of Erie County (New York) I introduced Lean Six Sigma four years ago and have transformed a bankrupt county into one of the most financially stable counties in America. Erie County is the largest upstate county in New York and home to the 3rd poorest city in the United States (Buffalo). Our remarkable progress can be attributed 80% to Lean and 20% to Six Sigma.

Lean is a lifetime journey – a journey well worth the time and energy it takes to understand and implement. Paul Akers provides just the right 'push' to get you started. So... get started!"

~Chris Collins - County Executive, Erie County, New York

"Every time I visit FastCap the people motivate me. The Lean culture is contagious. Like most places of employment, it comes down to the staff. If the people are on board and excited, it works."

~Caleb Erickson, Whatcom County Sheriff's Office

2 Second
Lean™

How to Grow People and
Build a Lean Culture

Fun

at Work
&
at Home

Paul A. Akers

FastCap Press

For information about special discounts for bulk purchases, please contact
Paul Akers: 888-443-3748 or paul@fastcap.com

Designed by Paul Akers
Fourth printing, May 2014
Over 20,000 Copies Sold
Manufactured in the United States of America

2 Second Lean comes in ALL flavors

You can read it...get even more insight by watching the video
links...and listen to the sound ideas of the expanded Audio-Book
with extra "off-script" inspiration and added stories of innovation.

	ISBN
2 Second Lean Printed Book	978-0-9846622-8-9
2 Second Lean eBook	978-0-9846622-2-7
2 Second Lean CD Audio-Book	978-0-9846622-1-0
2 Second Lean MP3 / iTunes Audio-Book Download	978-0-9846622-3-4

**Check out 2secondlean.com for these products
and all the latest Lean ideas!**

Acknowledgments

Editors
Angie Vogt, who edited the original manuscript.

Angela Thompson, for the final, final edits.

Special Thanks
Leanne Akers, my wife, for being by my side and building an amazing life and company with me.

Jon Lussier, for keeping FastCap® running smoothly while I buried my head in this project... and for all the great quotes.

The FastCap Team, for being the most amazing team of people anyone could ever work with.

Keith Turley, for publishing first and for kicking me in the butt to finish mine.

To an unknown Lean thinker
In 1998 I walked into a cabinet shop that looked totally different than any I had ever seen. There was no visible inventory, only one job was in process. Most of the machines were quiet and the work area was clean and highly organized. Work on that day was slow and the owner of the company was not in a panic, but simply instructed his people to perform maintenance throughout the facility. The company was successful, profitable and the people seemed to really enjoy their work. I walked out of that shop thinking, that guy is crazy. How can you make money and stay in business if your people are not producing product? Two years later I would learn the answer.

Contents

Find

What are QR Codes?
Look for these in the book!

Use your smartphone to scan any of the QR codes in this book...or just click on them...and they will take you directly to that Lean video or PDF!

All Lean Videos
http://bit.ly/xNSQoa

Our top Lean videos:

1. Lean Desk
http://youtu.be/-POV-VqEJIg

2. Morning Improvement Walk
http://youtu.be/3OEePS7Oh_g

Scan

3. Lean Problem Solving
http://youtu.be/gvIkPgf2eEE

Watch

4. Lean Burrito
http://youtu.be/uyzMQ2WwmWo

No QR Code Reader?
Find us on the web

1. Go to www.fastcap.com

2. Click on video tab

3. Lean Videos

All of FastCap's Lean videos are
100% FREE!

It's our way of paying it forward

Preface

Welcome to my world of Extreme Lean thinking. Once you have experienced the vast benefits of Lean, you will crave it, want it, and do anything to get it.

Because Lean thinking has made an enormous difference in my life – personally and professionally – I wanted the title of this book to convey how attainable it is to build a vibrant Lean culture. While there are many books on Lean, I have yet to find any that are fun. My mountain bike buddies would say, "It's SICK!" In fact, when I went looking for books or websites to recommend to people, all I found were books filled with complicated diagrams and business school theory-speak – definitely not the fun Lean that I have come to know and love.

This book is not intended for MBAs or those interested in manufacturing theory or flow charts. This book is intended to blast open the door of opportunity for people who want to improve their daily life, be it in their workplace or home. Lean is not as complicated as all the experts and textbooks make it out to be. In fact, as you learn to incorporate a Lean approach to your life, you will see that the more Lean thinking you have in your life, the more you will enjoy life.

Lean thinking has propelled my business from a small operation in my garage into an international, multi-million dollar enterprise. I have the most dedicated, fun-loving employees any business owner could hope for. I am living the American dream because someone shared with me the genius of Lean thinking. Like my Japanese mentors, I want to pass the gift of Lean thinking on to others, and create a more prosperous and productive culture around the world.

Lean thinking is fun and exciting! The ideas I have learned from my Lean friends are tectonic! I have attempted to write a Lean book - short, visual and simple.

Paul with his Lean Mentor VP of Hoks wearing Paul's Lear jet hat.

There are plenty of workshops, executive manuals and textbooks on the market. I wanted to write a book that would make Lean accessible to everyone, from homemaker to executive.

Our tour group at dinner with the President of Hoks, one of the best Lean companies that I visited in Japan.

As a personal habit, I read one book a week for my own intellectual development and I always play a little game after completing each book. I ask myself, "What is the one take-away that will rock my world if I seriously apply it?"

Boring Lean books that drone on and on! Lean should be fun!

I've incorporated this challenge at the end of every chapter, by adding a summary called "The One Thing." This summary will reinforce the main point(s) of each chapter in the leanest possible way. At any time you can quickly review and memorize the principles. So buckle up for a high-energy ride...as you begin to think and get Lean!

Lean thinkers build strong relationships surpassing all cultural barriers.

Chapter 1

What is Lean?

Ten years ago I began my Lean journey. I had never even heard the word before, but what happened was nothing short of astounding. My wife and I started our company, FastCap, in our garage in 1997. FastCap is a product development company that specializes in producing innovative tools and hardware for cabinetmakers and builders. Why woodworking products? Because I'm a passionate craftsman who lives and breathes for the opportunity to massage a piece of Honduras Mahogany.

Paul and Leanne in the early years of FastCap.

Our first product, the Fastcap, was a peel and stick cap to cover screw holes inside cabinets.

Paul in his shop at home.

Our second product was a laser-positioning tool called the Laserjamb. I had invented these products when I was a cabinetmaker. I figured out a way to manufacture and sell them to a market I was an expert in. (As an aside, my next book will be *How to Invent and Sell Your Genius.*)

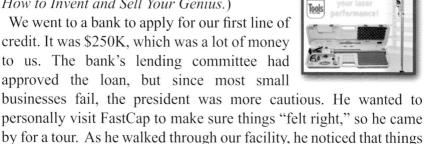

We went to a bank to apply for our first line of credit. It was $250K, which was a lot of money to us. The bank's lending committee had approved the loan, but since most small businesses fail, the president was more cautious. He wanted to personally visit FastCap to make sure things "felt right," so he came by for a tour. As he walked through our facility, he noticed that things were highly organized, we had a disciplined culture, and things ran very smoothly. After the tour he said to me, "Paul, I would loan you any amount of money you want. I have never been to a business so well run and organized. You really look like you know what you're doing."

Being the proud business owner, that was just about the highest compliment I could hope for. My wife Leanne and I had worked very hard at growing our business and had just won "Business Start-up of the Year" in Whatcom County.

Paul with the President of the Bank, "Son, you have a mighty fine business here..." :)

FastCap's Team in the early years.

Needless to say, the bank president's impression confirmed our feelings that we were doing extremely well. We were turning a good profit, our business was growing and our company had a young, hip, fast-paced culture. Everything looked and felt right. What could possibly be wrong with a profitable business that inspires such confidence from the local bank president? This raises the question, "Could a company with so much success have significant problems to address?"

We were having inventory problems, specifically with managing our incoming raw materials. I hired a manufacturing consultant to see if he could suggest a software program to manage our inventory more efficiently. After touring our entire facility I asked him, "So, Tracy, what do you think? Can you help me out?"

His reluctance was unnerving. He said, "Well, I don't know." I said, "Well, what do you think my problem is?" He paused, looked around the shop floor and said, "Do you want to know the truth?"

Managing thousands of colors of raw materials.

Tracy, the consultant that broke the news to me that we didn't know what we were doing.

I said, "Of course!" He said, "You don't know what you're doing and you don't know how to manufacture." Ouch.

A week earlier the bank president told me it was the best company he had ever seen and now this guy was telling me I didn't know what I was doing and that I was essentially in a free fall.

Paul... Free Falling!

To understand how hard these words hit me, you should know my background. Everything I had attempted in life up to this point I had not only achieved, but excelled at. I earned the rank of Eagle Scout at 14 and at 16 years old I built my first musical instrument and impressed guitar maker Bob

Paul's mentor, Bob Taylor, of Taylor Guitars.

Paul playing one of his custom built guitars.

Taylor so much that he hired me to work for Taylor Guitars™. I was lucky enough to be a part of building the first 2000 guitars that came out of that factory.

After graduating from college and with my background in manufacturing, I went on to become an Industrial Arts teacher and then was hired to manage a 100-unit condo development. It was a very complex construction project

Paul (the bearded guy) with his Industrial Arts Class.

and intimately tied to the manufacturing process. Also, I had been one of the lead builders for the home of the editor for Architectural Digest magazine, in Bel Air, CA and had restored many of the most beautiful historical homes in Pasadena, all in my early 20s.

Not only was I certain that I understood the principles of manufacturing, I had a rich background in manufacturing to prove it and an impressive list of accomplishments. And now, this guy, who I was paying to help me improve my business,

One of many of the historical homes I restored.

Paul's handbuilt craftsman home.

The Toyota Way
*One of Paul's favorite
books.*

was telling me I didn't know what I was doing.

Nevertheless, I humbled myself. "OK, Tracy, what do I need to do?" He said, "You need to learn something called TPS-Toyota Production System, also called Lean Manufacturing."

I asked "What is Lean?" I was about to find out.

THE ONE THING:
YOUR PRIDE WILL BLIND YOU TO WHAT YOU MOST NEED TO LEARN.

Lean Works for You

Identify the one thing you are really good at:

*Keeping track of promises/what I said
I'd do. Listening*

Surprise! It is probably where you have the most waste in your life and can apply Lean the most effectively.

Your thoughts and take-away from this chapter:

Lean videos:

1. What is Lean
http://youtu.be/_NYZzwqd01I

2. Lean in Government
http://youtu.be/tliTOVr1dkM

3. Paul Akers receives Seattle Magazine 2011 Executive of the Year
http://youtu.be/-337vqBIRrM

Chapter 2

You Mean I'm Really That Bad?

The very next week, after the infamous "you don't know how to manufacture" line, two kids named Brad and Jon showed up at our door. Brad and Jon had been missionary kids in Japan and had worked as translators for a Japanese man who was teaching Lean to American companies. They learned the concepts so well they decided to strike out on their own and my company, FastCap, was their first victim.

Brad translating for a Japanese Lean teacher.

Baby-faced kids, Brad and Jon, of Gemba Research, my original Lean teachers.

I was impressed by their observations, but their services came at a price that stunned me – $10,000 a week. I had a small business, not a bank. This was just out of my league, yet I knew I needed help if I wanted to grow my business to the next level. Something about their no-nonsense approach appealed to me. I put the full court press on my wife, and persuaded Leanne to let me spend the money. It has proven to be one of the most valuable decisions we have made. The journey was about to get serious. This would be like going from weekend basketball with the guys at work, to serious Olympic training. Routine or normal days were history.

Look at all the beautiful finished product..NOT!

They asked questions about everything, starting with, "Why are you making so much finished product?" I answered, "Because it takes so much time to set up the machine for each variation of our product. We might as well make a whole bunch of each type and then we can just pull from it as we need it over the next couple of months."

Brad and Jon told me that was waste because you have to stock,  inventory and manage all those goods. If you make just what you need, you don't have to stock, inventory and manage it all. That eliminates an enormous amount of waste. If the machine set-up time is holding you back, then find a way to set the machine up more quickly... instead of it taking 45 minutes, see if you can get that machine set-up time down to 5 minutes.

Brad with his winsome smile, "Paul, you have a lot to learn about Lean."

"Look," I said, "I could be your dad. I've been doing this for years. There is no way we are going to get that machine set up in 5 minutes and get it running with good parts." Brad smiled and said, "You have a lot to learn about Lean."

For the next week they observed our production process and evaluated everything we did from grabbing the dies, changing out tools faster, the distance we walked to access certain equipment  in the shop, to aligning the jigs and fixtures on our machines. Every step of the process was evaluated for efficiency and simplicity. We ended up making significant changes to cut down the machine set-up time, which then enabled us to easily produce the sizes, shapes, and colors according to specific customer orders rather than producing every possible variation in bulk.

Paul "eating crow"

Lo and behold, instead of 45 minutes and a great big hassle, we got the machine set-up process time down to 5 minutes. I was eating some serious crow. More importantly, to this day, we continue to improve the process, getting it down to as low as 2 minutes.

This was my introduction to Lean thinking. I was absolutely certain that Brad and Jon's ideas were impossible to achieve, yet right there before my eyes, in a matter of weeks, I saw the impossible materialize.

This first experience with Lean manufacturing introduced me to two foundational principles of Lean thinking: <u>eliminating waste</u> and <u>continuous improvement</u>.

While the bank manager was impressed with the appearance of a clean and organized shop, Brad and Jon immediately saw a shop floor of employees busily engaged in a cumbersome process that produced unnecessary inventory, which then required constant management and tracking. In order to eliminate the waste of excess inventory, we had to analyze our processes closely and find ways to improve them. Lean thinking presumes that everything can be improved continuously, without end. If you think that the idea of improvement is like going on vacation – something you do a couple times a year and then it's back to work – you are in for a big surprise.

After reading *The Toyota Way*, I came away with a new appreciation for just how radical the idea of "continuous improvement" really is. I now realize that wasted energy, wasted money, wasted resources and wasted time are continually pulling at us each and every day.

Toyota™ makes million of improvements every year, all generated from the ideas of their employees world wide!

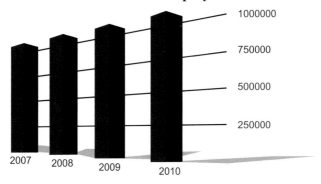

If you think you have your life or your business pretty well dialed-in, you're clueless. Toyota™ still makes millions of improvements worldwide to their processes and they have been thinking Lean for over 50 years. As my good friend and Lean buddy Jeff Kaas says, "Waste is like gravity; it pulls at you 24/7 and if you don't have a method to overcome it, you will lose and it will win!

THE ONE THING:
YOU AND I ARE 24/7 WASTE GENERATORS.

Lean Works for You

Start a journal and for one week keep track of all the activities and processes every day that <u>might</u> have waste in them.

At the end of the week see if there are more things that are wasteful than they are profitable, productive and efficient. The results might surprise you.

Your thoughts and take-away from this chapter:

Lean videos:

1. Lean Burrito
http://youtu.be/uyzMQ2WwmWo

2. Waste, waste, waste... it's everywhere
http://youtu.be/gFnSL29GHS0

3. Lean: The waste of waiting
http://youtu.be/ibBXtlco4ms

Chapter 3

One Piece Flow

The following weeks were like a religious retreat for me – an immersion into a new way of thinking. After my introduction to the power of eliminating waste and the concept of continuous improvement, I was introduced to the idea of "one-piece flow" or making one product at a time. This concept is about as counter-intuitive as it can get to the modern American mind. For the past century our culture has been steeped in a manufacturing economy that relies on mass production. We live in the era of "bigger is better," and "super-size me!" and "if something is good, more is better," right?

FastCap was no exception. We operated our shop floor in the mass production, big batch mode of thinking, which is exactly the opposite of one-piece flow.

At FastCap we produced large batches of products regardless of how many orders we had from customers, because we believed we were saving time and money. As it turned out, we were creating more work and mountains of waste using the batch production model.

We produced one of our products, called the Laserjamb™, in batches of 100. By our own calculations, it took about 45 minutes to produce each Laserjamb. A batch of 100 took about 75 work hours to complete from beginning to end. By producing them in batches of 100, we thought we were saving time, ensuring that we always had the product on hand to fill orders as they came in. When Brad and Jon suggested we start making these one at a time and only on a per-order basis, I thought they were out of

FastCap was hypnotized by big batch methodology of manufacturing.

their minds. I believe my actual words were, "No, that will never work!" (There's some saying about "teaching an old dog new tricks" that comes to mind right about now.)

The manufacturing environment I had created required enormous amounts of space dedicated toward making this product. Making them in batches of 100 meant that we needed to accommodate 100 Laserjambs for each step of the process. For starters, we needed enough workbench space to hold 100 Laserjambs at a time. This created a very spread-out situation that required transportation resources to move the Laserjambs from one part of the plant to another.

The old dog did indeed learn new impressive tricks!

The batch production process was consuming our space, equipment, personnel resources, and money. I looked at this as a necessary evil in exchange for efficiency. Making 100 at a time made the most sense to me. In humble compliance to Brad and Jon's recommendations, we started making one Laserjamb at a time. By any experienced manufacturer's first glance, this process would be too tedious and time-consuming to make sense. I was eager to show these so-called experts what a futile process this was going to be. I was humoring them, or so I thought.

Large workbenches to store large batches of work. If one mistake was made, the whole batch would need reworking.

Laserjambs new U-shaped Cell – one person doing the work of four with no mistakes.

They spent the first week re-arranging everything we did into small U-shaped manufacturing cells. My company started to look like some Asian revolution had just invaded and I was the victim. Remember how much confidence I had in my great company and my manufacturing ability? Well, it was nothing short of humiliating watching these young, "inexperienced" kids re-arrange almost everything about our company – stripping our shop floor to the most fundamental components. It was like somebody saying, "Paul, your baby is ugly. We'll take it from here." So much for my "young and hip" company!

What do you think happened? Once again my eyes were opened to the magic of Lean thinking. Using one-piece flow, each Laserjamb was produced from beginning to end by one person, who was able to visually inspect the whole piece as he or she was assembling it. This one-at-a-time process allowed us to catch mistakes as they were happening. Perhaps a hole was off-center or maybe a knob was not screwed on correctly. Whatever the mistake, we were able to catch it during the production process for each Laserjamb, rather than at the end of a batch. Fixing one defective Laserjamb is easy. Having to fix 100 defective Laserjambs at the end of a batch is a disaster!

Improvements like these had a transformative ripple effect as well. Not only did we see each product getting produced with more personalized care and attention – very few mistakes, if any – but the rest of the process began to go more smoothly as well. Filling the orders, loading, shipping, billing and the back and forth cash flow associated with this process was immediately simplified.

Rather than having 100 Laserjambs to store, inventory and track, we had zero because each Laserjamb was produced to fill an order. It was produced, packaged, boxed, shipped and paid for. This also meant that we weren't spending money producing something that hadn't been sold. We had a lot less inventory and labor hours sitting on the shelf. A good visual is to imagine all the finished goods as though they were heads of lettuce, wilting by the hour.

One-piece flow simplified and improved every other part of the manufacturing process. This Lean thinking was beginning to make sense to me, in a really counter-intuitive way.

Simple one-piece flow

> ## THE ONE THING:
> MAKE A BATCH AND WASTE WILL BE EVERYWHERE OR MAKE ONE, MAKE IT RIGHT AND WASTE WILL MAGICALLY DISAPPEAR.

Lean Works for You

Identify one area where you are currently doing batchwork:

_____

Time how long it takes you to make 10 products as a batch:
Your time: _____

Now, time yourself making one at a time until you reach 10:
Your time: _____

Your thoughts and take-away from this chapter:

Lean videos:

1. Lean FastCap Style
http://youtu.be/su9CulCZTBg

2. Lean Batchwork vs. One piece flow
http://youtu.be/mmop9huyYRU

3. Lean Cutter Change
http://youtu.be/i7klvrAm5gc

Chapter 4

It Only Gets Better From Here

My Lean journey was really taking hold of me. It was exhilarating going through this process of transformation. With each suggestion for improvement I would go through stages of disbelief and doubt, then humble resignation – only to be rewarded in complete and utter surprise as a simpler, more effective and less costly result unveiled itself before my eyes.

Our sink, before.

After - Faster, Simpler and Safer.

Since then, my critical eye has developed so that the waste component in everything we do at FastCap just leaps out at me. Even though I have been doing Lean for ten years and people travel from around the world to see and understand our Lean culture, I believe that 90% of everything we do is waste. Here are the eight wastes that plague us all. Number 8 is the greatest offender.

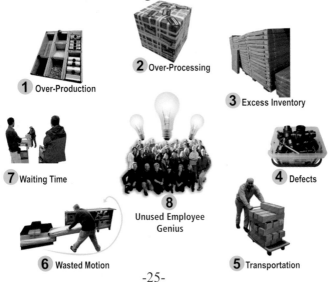

1 Over-Production
2 Over-Processing
3 Excess Inventory
4 Defects
5 Transportation
6 Wasted Motion
7 Waiting Time
8 Unused Employee Genius

Finding *the waste component is not a burden, it's a game – a giant scavenger hunt*. Lean does not make things more difficult. Lean is focused on intentionally simplifying any process. When you make a process simpler, you yield a better, more satisfying result with less effort. That point cannot be over-emphasized. Lean is not about working harder and more frantically, but about making things simpler. It is not just about making everything faster, but about improving the quality of everything you do. It's rarely a huge or drastic change, but small baby steps in an endless drive to continuously improve everything every day. Big changes are great, but it is not what Lean is all about.

I just shared how Lean was introduced into my business model and how it yielded dramatic results. The implications for how this thinking can affect one's personal life is nothing short of amazing.

| *A common work area that I see when I visit other companies. What a nightmare.* | *FastCap's workbench after 10 years of continuous improvement. What a dream.* |

If I haven't said it already (and I'll keep saying it!), Lean is about eliminating waste and about continuous improvement, by approaching everything you do with an eye toward making things simpler. If it takes an hour to do something, ask how it can be done in 30 minutes. It is not a frantic 30 minutes, it's 30 minutes you achieved by eliminating the 8 kinds of waste. Then when you get it down to 30 minutes, ask how you can get it down to 15 minutes. And after you reduce the time to just 7 minutes, get ready to do a happy dance. Before long you have eliminated the process altogether and sure jubilation will set in. Lean is the art of subtraction, not addition.

Lean is about continually reducing the waste stream that's involved in everything you do in your life – how you make your lunch in the morning or the way you get dressed in the morning. It can simplify how you collect your car keys and briefcase before you go to work, how you get the kids ready in the morning, family meal time, yard work, home maintenance – it doesn't matter. Lean thinking applies to every aspect of life and therefore can improve every aspect of life. Yes, becoming a Lean thinker makes everything in life a little bit better!

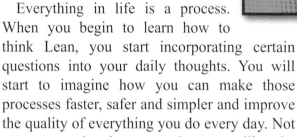

Drawers are labeled, Dishwasher step by step buttons and a red and green hook and loop dot to identify clean or dirty.

Everything in life is a process. When you begin to learn how to think Lean, you start incorporating certain questions into your daily thoughts. You will start to imagine how you can make those processes faster, safer and simpler and improve the quality of everything you do every day. Not once, not twice, but every day you will make small improvements for the rest of your life.

That's what we mean by increasing the quality of your life, your business and your general outlook on life. Can you imagine every day

Even the Salt and Pepper shakers have a home. :)

everything getting a little bit better? Not dramatically, but consistently getting better? When you become a Lean thinker this is what happens and it is a massively fulfilling way to live!

IMPROVE THE PROCESS
- THE 8 WASTES
LEAN THINKING

> ## THE ONE THING:
> ### FINDING THE WASTE COMPONENT IS NOT A BURDEN, IT'S A GAME – A GIANT SCAVENGER HUNT.

Lean Works for You

Look around you and identify one example of the 8 wastes in your life:

1. Over Production: _____

2. Over Processing: _____

3. Excess Inventory: _____

4. Defects: _____

5. Transportation: _____

6. Wasted Motion: _____

7. Waiting Time: _____

8. Not Using Employee Genius: _____

Lean videos:

1. Lean Kitchen
http://youtu.be/Ui-Lk6gK7m8

Chapter 5

What Bugs You?

Let me give you some examples of how I've implemented Lean at home, not just at work. I have a closet, and when I go into that closet every morning, there are about ten different suits that I wear, as well as my casual clothes and sportswear. The problem is that I'm 50 years old and I'm blind as a bat and I can no longer distinguish the different colors with ease.

Before and after. My Lean improvement to my closet – installing voluminous lights so I can finally color match with confidence. Why did I wait 16 years!!

When I built the house 16 years ago, I installed a light in the closet. It still works fine, but my eyes don't. With one light you get shadows and dark corners, which means every morning is a struggle. I found myself pulling a suit out of my closet (not my polyester powder blue suit) and walking into the center of my bedroom under the brighter light in order to match a shirt and tie. After so many trips to and from the closet, I realized how tedious this had become. The process of getting dressed was bugging me! What would happen if I put two or three more fluorescent lights in there? There would be no more shadows or dark corners! That was my next weekend project.

Today my closet is illuminated as though God were talking to me in the morning! When I turn on

Before and after. Entry coat closet. It was single rod, now double with my wife's coats on top in the choice position. I installed lights down below so I could see. It is almost an afterlife experience there is so much light.

that light switch, I can see every little nuance of color differentiation between my suits, my clothes, my shirts and my pants. Now, starting my day with something as routine as getting dressed no longer frustrates me or slows me down. These little victories are psychologically liberating. They sound like such small things, but when you simplify a necessary daily process from a tedious back and forth effort into an easy set of options, life gets really good, really fast. No more walking back and forth, no more guessing, no more mistakes, no more rework, no more hassle.

I had been suffering for 16 years with the problem and never

My friend, Karl Wadensten, who makes Vibrators... for concrete. ;) Karl is one of the best Lean thinkers I have ever met and his company is filled with people who are passionate about being at war with waste.

solved it. With one moment of recognition ("this process really bugs me") and a commitment to fixing it (the weekend project), I improved one of the first processes I perform every day for the rest of my life.

Lean is about fixing what bugs you. I learned this concept from Karl Wadensten from VIBCO™. Karl is another one of those rare Lean thinkers who makes Lean both simple and fun. He runs a big company in Providence, Rhode Island that makes industrial vibrators... for bulk material handling and concrete! :) Karl has a radio show called *The Lean Nation* and runs around his company wearing a pith helmet, declaring, "We are at war with waste." He's one of my best Lean buddies and he turned me on to this concept. Remember, "Lean is simply fixing what bugs you."

Arthur(79) and Henry(80) of VIBCO. They affectionately refer to themselves as "Re-treads." They are in their second careers at VIBCO and are huge contributors to the Lean culture, called upon to contribute daily to solve problems through their wealth of experience.

What bugged me was I couldn't

see my clothes in my closet. So I took action and I made it happen. Now, for the rest of my life, I enjoy the experience of getting dressed in the morning with good lighting as I look over my choices. Not to mention, I got some "honey-do" points because my wife shares the same closet and now she can see her clothes better as well. Everybody wins – another benefit of Lean.

I have literally made hundreds of Lean improvements in my home, but let me share with you one of my favorites. In the morning, I make tea. I like to put in a little pack of Splenda™, some cinnamon, and then my tea. I do this every morning. The process is straight forward enough. I open the drawer, pull out a pack of Splenda™, tear it open, dump it in my teacup, turn around, walk to the trash, and I put the empty Splenda pack in the trash. I then put a shot of cinnamon in my cup, and put the cinnamon away. I put in the tea bag, walk over to the hot water tap, put the hot water in, and I am done.

Actually, I don't like having to tear those packs of Splenda open. I have been doing it for years, and it drives me crazy. One day I decided to buy Splenda in bulk. I bought a little sugar shaker and put the Splenda in it. After that, my routine changed slightly. I would take my cup out, one shot of Splenda, one shot of cinnamon, put the tea bag in, put the hot water in, and I was done.

I saved myself about five seconds, not having to deal with

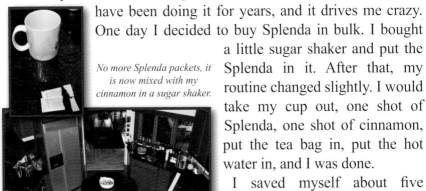

No more Splenda packets, it is now mixed with my cinnamon in a sugar shaker.

Lean solution! Eliminating wasted motion. No more walking back and forth to make my tea. Walking is waste. Fast and Easy!

Tea and Splenda-cinnamon mix are right by the hot water tap.

3 Teas Per Day Savings Breakdown

Time: 30 seconds per day = 3 hours per year.

Distance: 10 steps per tea x 3 teas per day = 30 steps saved per day = 32,850 feet per year = 6 miles less traveled.

the tearing open of the Splenda pack. I know you think it's a small thing, but it's the small things that add up to big things. Next, I thought to myself, "I'm the only one that uses cinnamon and Splenda in the house, so why not just take the cinnamon and put it in the Splenda shaker?"

Again, my routine was simplified. Now I gave one shake of Splenda-cinnamon mix, then put the tea bag in the hot water and I was done without making a single step. I saved myself ten seconds every day for the rest of my life. Of course, I make about three or four cups of tea a day. So, multiply ten seconds three times, and see how making tea is now a breeze and gets me out the door that much faster.

In addition though, think about all the other waste I have eliminated on a more global level. There are lots of processes involved. There's the process of getting Splenda in those packets and the waste involved in the labor and production that goes into making the little paper packets. Somebody has to make, print and transport those packets, then deliver the final product to the store. Somebody has to inventory it in the store. I have to buy it, take it home and put it in my drawer. Then I use it and throw it out. Then the garbage truck has to pick it up and haul it to the landfill, and the landfill guy has to plow it under, and then the landfill has to be managed.

There is a lot of waste associated with that one act, and yet it happens billions of times a day all over the world, not just with Splenda, but with lots of things. And now, I've eliminated all of that. I don't have to waste that paper. I don't have to cut down that tree. Lean is really the ultimate green vehicle.

I'll give you two more examples of what I've done in my home, though I could go on and on and on. This one, though, is a favorite for all of us who hate the clean up after mowing the lawn.

I have to mow my lawn every week, like most of us do. I have two acres to mow, so I use a large commercial lawn mower. I used to bag my grass all the time, but that was a lot of time and a lot of waste, because I was getting off the mower to empty the bag several times during the process.

Somebody once suggested that I try mulching it. I said I didn't really want to because the lawn doesn't look as good after mulching. Well, I learned that if I mowed the lawn a little taller,

Instead of my yards being overwhelming to maintain, I make continuous Lean improvements which make maintaining it fun and easy.

and got less clippings, my lawn would actually start looking better in the long run. So, I started mulching it. Now I have to fertilize

Pull my Handle! You know you want to!

Water features are for lawn mowers, too! Many practical jokes have been played on my friends by telling them to pull the handle.

less because the mulched grass is actually a lot healthier for the lawn. I saved money and time by not having to fertilize half as much as I used to. Whether I bagged or mulched the grass when I finished mowing the lawn, I had to actually go and spray off and clean the bottom of the mower deck because grass would get packed on the blades underneath. (I live in the Pacific Northwest where we mow even when it rains.) This was a big hassle and a lot of work. I would have to get off my lawn mower, take a hose, stick it underneath the mower and clean under the deck of the mower. It was a very labor intensive process. I didn't like doing it. What would happen if I laid a pipe on the ground, drilled holes in it and hooked a garden hose up to where there's a little on/off diverter switch? I would be able to drive the mower over the pipe, turn the little knob and let the water spray up evenly under the entire deck.

Lawn Mower Bidet! Even my lawn mower gets thrilled about Lean!

The treated 4x4 posts contain the grass clippings, the pressure washer is set up and ready to clean the underside of the mower. The water will shoot 25 feet in the air at full pressure. Kids love to play in it too!

Big yards and big jobs require big Lean thinking!

Well, I tried it and guess what? It worked. It saved me a lot of time. I no longer had to get on and off the lawn mower!

Lean is a process of continuous improvement, right? I didn't like how the hose and pipe contraption looked in my equipment area. So, I took it one step further. What if I built that little pipe into the concrete, cut out a little hole, put the pipe down in there, put the concrete back over the top, so only little holes were visible in the concrete? Again, I just drove up, pulled the lever back and the water sprayed up out of the concrete. My deck cleaning system was camouflaged. It was clean - no hose and pipe contraption lying around to clutter up my work area. It was seamless. Well, I did it, and you know what, it works fabulously! My friends just drool over this cool mechanism I've built. Why? Because it's actually cool and fun! This is Lean thinking.

Now when I finish my lawn, it's easy (and fun) to clean off the bottom of the deck. I feel good about the continual improved state of my home.

Now, my last example of Lean improvement in the home is one of my favorites as well, because it's so simple.

My two children, 16 and 18 years respectively, like to eat toast. They make toast and – being teenagers – they leave that butter knife sitting on the counter. Frankly, this habit was driving me crazy for some time. It didn't matter how much I harangued them to put the butter knife on the edge of the dish or in the dishwasher. Oh, for a day or two it would be remedied because my kids are good kids and they do listen to me (really, they do)! Soon enough, though, that knife would start showing up again, leaving crumbs and butter on the counter.

So one day I asked myself "Why does the butter knife always end up on the counter?" The answer is because the butter knife doesn't sit very long on the edge of the butter dish. It just falls off. So, I wondered, what would

The infamous floating butter knife, Paul's butter brush to the rescue!

happen if I used a paintbrush to butter my toast? I went over to the kitchen drawer, opened it up and found this really cute pastry brush that was round with short little stout bristles and very attractive. I took it over, and I put it in the soft butter and the brush stands up perfectly in soft butter. I made a piece of toast to test this idea out, and lo and behold, it worked perfectly. The butter brush stuck in the butter, so it didn't fall out very easily, and it looked nice, standing straight up in the little butter dish. So when I came home that evening, my daughter said, "Hey Papa! That butter brush is so cool. It's so easy." That's the power of Lean thinking. It works and people recognize it works because life is simplified, made easy, and something that had really been bugging me was resolved.

Now there's a critical point I want to make here. Lean is really about removing those things that bug you. This is the way I teach Lean because it's a fun starting point. People can understand and identify with all the things in their lives that bug them and drive them crazy. Also, people enjoy being asked, "What bugs you?" The shy ones might not offer anything at first, but I guarantee you they will start thinking about it and before long they will be just as engaged in the process as you.

When we reduce the Lean concepts down to simple ideas like this, everybody wins. This is why Lean works everywhere it is tried – at home and at work. The quality of life can improve. Just ask yourself every day, "What bugs me?" I guarantee you, your answers will surprise you.

THE ONE THING:
YOU ARE AT WAR WITH
WHAT BUGS YOU!

Lean Works for You

List 5 things that bug you at home:
1. _____
2. _____
3. _____
4. _____
5. _____

List 5 things that bug you at work:
1. _____
2. _____
3. _____
4. _____
5. _____

Lean videos:

1. Lean at Home 1
http://youtu.be/3FOR9iOH2_c

Chapter 6

Domo Arigoto, Mr. Lexus!

Now I'd like to return to Lean in the workplace because, like all journeys, my Lean journey hit a rough patch. I see this everywhere I go in the manufacturing and corporate world. For some people the very word "Lean" earns a frown or at the very least a look of dread. These are the people who tried Lean and hit the same rough patch I did. This rough patch is a sign that the practitioner doesn't fully understand the comprehensive nature of Lean. My two trips to Japan over a five-year period finally gave me the full appreciation of Lean thinking and the motivation to implement it effectively.

Why isn't this working like they said it would?

In the early days of the journey, my impression of Lean was that it was a very promising business tool that would help my company expand and grow into a more efficient and sophisticated operation. Using Lean as *only* a tool will leave you disappointed. It is much more than that.

The first three months took me through a whiplash of emotions. The changes, hard as they were to accept, brought significant rewards – saving the company tens of thousands of dollars and bringing a fresh air of efficiency and simplicity to FastCap. And that was in just three months!

I felt like a new man...like I had accomplished something significant.

I've done it! Time to celebrate!

It was time for the consultants to go home, now that I knew what I was doing, right? Mmmm, not so fast!

These so-called "tremendous" changes I had undergone were actually considered very small in the eyes of my mentors. When I told them of my plans to build a larger facility, they looked at me like I was crazy. "Why?

You have too much already!" they protested. I still didn't get it.

It was at this time that Brad and Jon suggested that I participate in a new program. I would travel with several other business leaders to Japan for an immersion training experience in Lean manufacturing. Part of the excursion included an up-close and personal orientation to the Toyota Production System (TPS). How could I say NO? Japan is The Holy Land, the mother country, of Lean thinking. Of course I said YES!

That first pilgrimage to Japan was like an avalanche of learning and inspiration. I was overwhelmed with more information and impressions

My first trip to Japan with Brad and Jon from Gemba Research.

Lean from their work spaces to their manufacturing...

than I could possibly process. The production facilities were institutions of efficiency and simplicity. It was like watching one person accomplish the job of ten in the cleanest, most organized spaces I had ever seen. I didn't know how I was going to relay all this new information back to my people, but I came away convinced that Lean would solve many of the problems I was having at FastCap.

When I returned I implemented more improvements and began initiating what are called Kaizen events. A Kaizen event is when a group of employees focuses on a process and

These people are dialed in! Even her coat is ironed.

examine every step, then put it back together – removing all the non-value activity or waste. It's a team approach to making improvements.

For the next few years FastCap saw many improvements. We cut a lot of waste, simplified processes and saw our business grow steadily. I have to admit, though, Lean manufacturing started to feel like a grind. I noticed that I had become the sole driving force behind our Lean implementation. As long as I was around to initiate ideas or to lead brainstorming sessions or Kaizen events, we'd see progress. As soon as I walked away or took a business trip, things just seemed to linger where they were left. It was like pushing a train. When I meet people that have implemented Lean it is common for them to feel frustrated because they can't get Lean to really take root in their company.

I believe this may be the point

What a contrast! Stacks of batchwork before and now fast and simple one piece flow! Building just what you need when you need it. One piece flow is counterintuitive. Batchwork seems faster and more efficient but it is just the opposite. In this picture we show one of our many U-shaped Lean cells throughout our facility.

at which many people give up on Lean. I am eternally grateful that I didn't give up, because what happened on my second pilgrimage to Japan was a watershed moment in how I understood the big picture. I discovered the critical missing link in my methods and why I was not able to make Lean thinking "stick." I needed to get beyond the "doing Lean events" grind and this second pilgrimage to Japan gave me just the perspective I needed.

The highlight of this second trip was a tour of the Lexus™ plant and a two-hour lecture by the Vice-President of Lexus. The Lexus facility was one of the most elegant and fascinating models of production I had ever seen. At the

On the bus on our second tour of Japan.

end of the tour I asked the Vice President a very direct question, "What is the most important thing for Toyota?"

The most important thing for Toyota™ is people – teaching and training people in a culture of continuous improvement.

I was hoping for an answer besides the obvious, "eliminating waste through continuous improvement" response, given that those are the pillars of Lean manufacturing. I desperately needed to hear something different, something more inspiring, though I had no idea what that would be. The VP did not disappoint.

Without hesitating he said, "The most important thing for Toyota is people. Toyota is all about teaching and training people and building a culture of continuous improvement. We don't care about the next hybrid, the next engineering marvel, not even the next sales strategy. Our number one concern is how to build our people and how to build a culture of continuous improvement." This was hardly the answer I expected, but it was my "Eureka!" moment for the trip.

I had just spent the last five years focusing on waste and continuous improvement. Toyota, on the other hand, was obsessed with building a culture through teaching and training its people. In contrast, I was trying to convince my people to embrace Lean thinking by initiating "Lean events." My mistake had to do with my incorrect focus on processes. I needed to focus on building a culture of people who understand and embrace continuous improvement.

My misguided, but hopeful, intent was that my employees would see this marvelous process of identifying waste and continuous improvement with the same excitement that I did. If they experienced the Lean process through my eyes, I just knew they would adopt it with the same vigor and enthusiasm. My conversation with the Lexus VP made me realize that my understanding of what Lean is and how Lean works was flawed.

Endless teaching, training and building a culture of continuous improvement.

The problem was one of motivation. I was motivated as a business owner who wanted to see my business grow and expand successfully. Implementing

Lean principles was helping me get to that goal of a well-run company. My employees, however, were motivated by the usual things that keep people coming to work, such as a good job, a paycheck, personal satisfaction, and a sense of camaraderie with other employees. They were not necessarily motivated by my grand business plan!

Now it was clear to me that my primary task was to go home and build a culture of Lean thinking by focusing on growing people. "Building a Lean culture" was the missing link for me, and it's why I couldn't get the improvements at FastCap to "stick." It's the reason I felt like I was pushing a train. Lean is about building a culture of continuous improvement, not about conducting Lean events.

Like any other aspect of self-improvement, the hardest part is not learning how to do it. The hardest part is changing the culture, the lifestyle, so that progress is an ongoing, permanent upward course. We all know someone who lost weight or started a new positive habit like exercise, meditation or daily prayer. We also know that a year later many of these life improvements tend to drop off. We are creatures of habit. Change is an easy experiment, but a bad habit is like a jealous, abandoned mistress – constantly vying for our return!

My foray into Lean was no exception. Not only did I need to incorporate this new way of thinking as a permanent and progressive change of habit, but I needed my craftsmen, warehouse employees, shipping and packaging people, office managers and executive directors to embrace this way of thinking. I wasn't sure how I would accomplish that, but what happened next on this Japanese pilgrimage sure pointed me in the right direction!

On my way home with a new understanding, new determination and a new goal.

THE ONE THING:
AT IT'S CORE, LEAN IS REALLY ABOUT THE PROCESS OF GROWING PEOPLE.

Lean Works for You

Name five things you are doing currently to grow people that you have influence over:

1. _____
2. _____
3. _____
4. _____
5. _____

Name one thing you are going to start doing tomorrow to grow people:

_____

Lean videos:

1. Lean Lexus
http://youtu.be/Wa1sAR1aYzo

2. FastCap Company Goals, PDF file
http://bit.ly/xMn1R4

Chapter 7

Let's Think Like Hoks!

After leaving Lexus, our next stop was Hoks, a company that specializes in making electronic circuitry. Brad told us that of all of the companies we would visit on our tour of Japan, Hoks would be the ultimate model of how Lean thinking can transform a business. With $100 million a year in sales, Hoks is actually considered a small company.

Located in the southern part of Japan, Hoks is an inspiring success story of a company that defied all odds by turning

Early 7 am at Hoks

an annual loss of $10 million to an annual profit of $10 million. How? By implementing a Lean strategy, I mean a Lean culture! I was looking forward to this visit and learning from someone who had come from the brink of bankruptcy to towering success.

We arrived at seven o'clock in the morning, dressed business casual and no doubt expecting the same royal treatment we received from Lexus. There we stood, waiting for the lecture and the tour. The president, Mr. Manabe, greeted each of us with a brush and a bucket.

On hands and knees, the president of Hoks performing the same 3S chores as team members. If you are like me, you are probably thinking to yourself, there has to be a more efficient way to do this... The purpose of this exercise was not efficiency, but humility.

He then proceeded to gesture us all on the floor, along with the other company executives, down on our hands and knees – that's right – to scrub the floor. Now this was a new level of Lean that I had never seen before and as you can imagine we were all a little shocked!

The president of Hoks was going to demonstrate for us one of the basic tenets of Lean, which is 5S-ing. First I need to give you a very quick primer.

There are five principles of Lean that business leaders are taught. These things, referred to as "The 5Ss of Lean," are a basic starting point for those who are new to Lean thinking. The "5Ss" are:

1. **Sort** - sort everything and remove what is not necessary to the job at hand and get rid of all the clutter and junk.

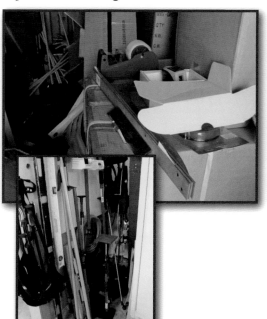

2. **Straighten** - a way to prioritize and organize the tools and resources needed for efficiency so that employees have easy access to their tools or supplies.

3. Shine - a clean environment improves morale and actually makes it easier to identify equipment deterioration and/or malfunction .

4. Standardize - this involves building consensus in the workplace for best practices so that everybody understands what to expect and what is expected of them.

5. Sustain - finding ways to keep the changes in place. It is easier than you think if everything has a place and every place has a thing. I mean everything, even the salt and pepper.

Now back to the story of our Hoks tour. We were all on our hands and knees scrubbing the floor with the president of Hoks and his company executives. The president and director, Mr. Emoto, shared with us what it was like in the dark days when their company was facing bankruptcy. His decision to build a Lean culture was a last-ditch effort to save the company. Feeling overwhelmed by the 5Ss, he decided to implement just three: sweeping, sorting, and standardizing everything. This man truely had a gift for simplifying things. He understood that if you made things simple, there was a much greater chance of people understanding and implementing the ideas. 5S-ing became 3S-ing.

Mr. Emoto sharing the story of Hoks while on the shop floor.

Every morning at 7 o'clock his employees showed up to sweep, sort, and standardize. They did this without pay, because they were motivated to save the company. In the process of engaging in these 3Ss, a type of

All hands on deck, 3S-ing at Hoks. Every morning and everyone.

bonding among the company employees took place. The 3Ss were simple and the results satisfying enough that a sense of accomplishment and ownership began to take hold.

The president of Hoks had learned about Lean and began to implement it in the simplest way he knew how. It demonstrated that a small improvement, even baby steps towards improvement can pay off in big ways. What took hold of the employees was a type of compounding effect.

As they cleaned, sorted and standardized, they unloaded mountains of waste that were lowering their productivity. We were shown pictures of excess tables, chairs and equipment

None of us really understands how much junk is impeding our effective work.

that were removed from all the work areas – mountains of waste that filled their entire back parking lot. The turn around, from $10 million in the red to $10 million in profit, is nothing short of miraculous, but it happened as a result of a super simple plan of implementing three of the 5Ss!

The momentum became addictive and everyone involved began to carry a sense of pride because they knew it was critical to the survival of their company and integral to its ongoing success. The leadership wore the same uniform, scrubbed the same floor, and worked at the same stand-up desk as everyone else. Everyone was respected and treated as

Above: The Hoks team having lunch in their blue uniforms.
Right: Working efficiently at their stand-up desks.

equals. Everyone engaged in continuous improvement, which brought more ideas and more engagement. Every morning before they ever worked it was company-wide 3S-ing. At 8 o'clock, the president of the company called everyone together and they played some cute Japanese music and did stretching exercises. Then he talked with them about important issues and principles regarding the company, and an hour and a half after employees first arrived for the day, everyone began to work on the actual manufacturing of Hoks products. Even after the company had recovered, Hoks employees proudly practiced the 3Ss on a daily basis. Also noteworthy was that Hoks was competing very well against a comparable product from a Chinese company, even though Hoks had 17 times the labor costs as the Chinese company. A Lean strategy will always yield a simpler, safer and better product, and with happier, very involved employees!

The time invested in people and their work environment is critical to the success of Lean. Hoks is a shining example of that ethic and they have enjoyed the success that comes with the discipline to sustain what they believe in.

There were many other memorable things that we saw at Hoks. The most surprising thing was that everything was on wheels, including their desks! All their desks were made from "Gemba" pipe (meaning "shop floor"), which made for a simpler, more flexible desk that was much taller. Another striking feature about these desks was that nobody sat at them! Everyone stood. There were a few chairs around but we rarely saw them used.

Even President Manabe's stand-up desk is on wheels!

Everything was labeled and outlined, and I mean everything, including every electrical outlet light switch and clock. It was amazing the sense of order and discipline, like nothing I have ever seen.

Desks raised, plants, filing cabinets, everything is on wheels and easily mobile.

The waiting room furniture was on wheels.

Heavy racking on wheels.

After an extensive jaw dropping tour through their facility and then a two-hour lecture by the Hoks president, I approached him, just like I had with the Lexus VP. I asked him what happens when other companies like Nissan™, Ford™, Chrysler™, and other Japanese companies come to see what his company has accomplished.

He looked at me and said, "Paul, smart people can't believe it could be this simple." There it was in living color – my take-away lesson about the grind I was fighting at FastCap. If you feel like you're pushing a train or like you're spinning your wheels trying to make Lean work, then you're doing it all wrong.

Lean is simple to the core. You will dramatically increase the odds of failure if you overcomplicate it. It is not the maze of complex flow charts and processes that today's consultants try to push on companies. In fact, the president of Hoks had reduced the most basic Lean checklist from 5Ss to 3Ss and made it so simple that 100% of the team could understand and achieve the goals. A consistent disciplined approach to continuous improvement is the gasoline that makes the engine run.

The President of Hoks made his facility easy to understand through strong visual controls. He immediately involved the employees in the process of sorting and organizing their own workplace and the end result was the survival and prospering of his company. This was because he created a culture of improvement, using the 3Ss as the framework for success.

Lean

Not Lean

FastCap's general manager, Jon Lussier, had accompanied me on this second trip to Japan. We immediately began to plan and strategize. I now understood that we needed to take FastCap from the level of "doing Lean events" to building a Lean culture. How would we build a Lean culture in Bellingham, Washington? How could we recreate the Hoks culture at FastCap? One of our goals was to actually look like Hoks within one year. We were light years from that goal, but we believed that with a new focus on building culture, anything was possible. This raises the next question and the topic of our next chapter: How does one build a Lean culture?

Jon and I reaching our goal and climbing Mt. Whitney, 14, 494 feet. Next we headed home to achieve our goal of building a lean culture.

THE ONE THING:
SMART PEOPLE CAN'T BELIEVE IT CAN BE THIS SIMPLE

Lean Works for You

What things have you been over-complicating?

What are the top three things you need to simplify for your team to succeed:

1. _____

2. _____

3. _____

Note: I realized I needed to focus on my ineffective training and leadership style. I had a strong tendency to blame the employees instead of realizing most of the problems stemmed from ineffective leadership, poor processes and bad training.

Lean videos:

1. Art of Subtraction
http://youtu.be/QZUPPQ7tGx4

2. Keeping the Rope Tight
http://youtu.be/nYDSC7zWMxl

Chapter 8

Let's Build a Lean Culture

I hope by now I have demonstrated how Lean thinking can transform a business and a home. You should have a sense that Lean is focused on the concepts of eliminating waste through continuous improvement and that it all begins with the simple question, "What bugs me?" I've also discussed how Lean can become a grind when we are focused on just the process, instead of the people. In fact, I believe this is the point where most people give up on Lean, they are 90% process focused and 10% people focused. When in reality, it should be 100% the opposite.

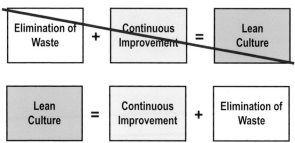

I came away from my second trip to Japan with the clear conviction that in order for Lean to work in the long term and to "stick," I would have to build a Lean culture. Without a doubt, this is the biggest challenge – how does one build a culture of continuous improvement? How do you get people to always look for ways to improve?

Well, I have to admit I was as ignorant about this as anybody. I saw a shining display of Lean culture at Hoks and that was how I wanted my company to look. I knew it had to be simple so that everybody at FastCap, from the shop floor to the office managers, could buy into it. I also knew it had to be sustainable, something that could become a natural way of thinking that would support and even reinforce our company and employees' belief systems.

Our belief systems were simple. We wanted continuous improvement, a focus on quality and the elimination of waste at every turn.

FastCap's Morning Meeting.
- *Review Mistakes*
- *Review Improvements*
- *Sales Numbers*
- *FastCap Principles*
- *Raving Fan Letters*
- *Product Training*
- *History Lesson*
- *Stretching*

We started the effort by imitating what we saw at Hoks, and began with what we refer to as the morning meeting. At 8 o'clock every morning we committed a very short time, maybe five or ten minutes, to gathering together before any production work could begin. We started with the most basic things, such as reading aloud the daily sales and reviewing the mistakes we made from the day before. We would open the floor to suggestions on how to prevent those mistakes and what new processes we might need to consider for improvement. Finally, we reviewed any new processes introduced from the day before and evaluated the effectiveness of those new methods. Those were the three or four things that we did consistently every day.

Then we had an idea. My wife, Leanne, realized how much the books we read influenced us. We were always reading some new book on the market and on a daily basis we'd find time to discuss them. They were usually about business, self-improvement or history. Our

Continuous learning for everyone is the backbone of a Lean Culture.

general manager, Jon, was also an avid reader and the three of us often talked between ourselves and reviewed what we learned and liked (or didn't like) about each book. Some of our favorites have been, *Good to Great*, and *Built to Last: Successful Habits of Visionary Companies* by Jim Collins. We also liked *Built From Scratch* (the Home Depot story). As company leaders, reading and discussing the principles from these best sellers gave us a point of reference for problem solving. It dawned on us that maybe involving the whole company in reading these books would help to unify our perspective. After all, we were trying to create a culture of problem-solvers. In

Small sample of FastCap's library. Smart educated people can solve any problem.

fact, my goal was to create a culture of the best problem-solvers in the world (literally), so it made sense to share these pearls of wisdom from some of the most visionary business leaders in the world. We thought they should be shared with everyone at FastCap.

So we incorporated into our morning meeting a bit of reading out loud from these great books. We would discuss certain highlights we came across and open the floor for discussion or comments. Even though we only read two or three pages a day, we were committed to this concept of learning together. We went through so many books. Some favorites were *Raving Fans* and *The Purple Cow*. We were relentless in our commitment to this process and as a result, it allowed all of our people to be on the same page as our management team.

Our morning meeting had evolved from just five or ten minutes into thirty to forty-five minutes as we reviewed the sales numbers, the mistakes, the improvements, and shared a few book club pages for reflection and consideration. Before long, our team members started thinking the way we thought since we were now literally on "the same page!" We were introducing our employees to world class ideas and innovative leaders in the business world.

Then we branched from self-improvement and business books into history. I love history, so I started to encourage our people to consider things from a historical perspective. How did people in the past solve problems? What were the factors that they considered before they solved the problem? This kind of critical thinking became

The key to teaching history is to make it fun and interesting. There is an endless supply of high quality historical videos that will energize and fascinate even the biggest history haters among us... Make it fun!

integral to building a culture of continuous improvement.

The first three months were hard work. It was like pulling teeth to keep everybody enthusiastic or even interested. We didn't get everybody on-board and some thought maybe we were a little crazy. Why were we "wasting" this first hour of the day not building product? Why were we standing around in a circle in this crazy morning meeting? But after three months, things started to look pretty positive and then after six months, because we didn't give up (just like a good diet), things really started looking good. After one year, we were on fire.

We were putting our money where our mouth was, so to speak. We weren't just talking about continuous improvement, we were teaching our people what it looked like on a daily basis. The first year we implemented the morning meeting and it grew and it morphed and it continually got better.

As good as the morning meeting became, we made one more significant change after the first year. The meeting was always

People you would never expect to speak in front of large groups become proficient and comfortable as a morning meeting leader.

led by either me or Jon, my general manager. As demands on our time grew with our expanding business, we found that there were times when neither of us could be there because of our travel schedules. It was very difficult for the meeting and the substance of the meeting to be maintained in our absence.

We decided we needed to teach our people how to lead a meeting and what better way to do it than let them experience it? Now we were really beginning to walk the talk! We decided that not only would someone else lead the meeting in our absence, but also on a daily basis; we would rotate the duties of morning leader among our employees. We appointed a new person to be a leader every day. So now we're not only teaching people about continuous improvement, but we're training people to be leaders. We took people who were as shy as church mice, who would never have spoken in front of a group of people before, and we nurtured and trained them to do something they never thought they could do.

Well, guess what? Did they feel good about themselves? They felt fabulous about themselves, because they came to work every day and they saw personal improvement as well as

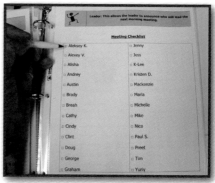
Building leaders one check mark at a time.

improvement in their work environment and their work situation. This is the beginning of how we built a culture of continuous improvement. We build leaders every day at FastCap.

During this tremendous curve in our company culture, my friend, Jeff Kaas, who was also working on building a Lean culture in his business, introduced me to a powerful concept.

He said, "Paul, if you want your people to move to the next level, start letting people tour your facility."

I thought that sounded like a real challenge. Are we good enough to have others look to us as an example of Lean in action?

Jeff said, "When you're on stage all the time and when outsiders come to look at what you're doing, your people will naturally want to live up to that expectation. They will get better and better by default."

So, we began inviting and allowing

Jeff Kaas of Kaas Tailored, aircraft interior manufacturers. Lean teacher extraordinaire, Jeff gives two Learn to See Tours a week.

other companies to tour our facility. What better way to show them our continuous improvement efforts? This proved to have other benefits that I never expected.

Our people felt good about the fact that other people wanted to see what they were doing. As I discovered in human behavior, the number one thing that everybody really wants in life is to be recognized and told they are doing a good job. By inviting others to come and observe our company we were saying to the world, "Look at what great things we do!" It was like putting your best project on display for the Science Fair judges!

The best way to move Lean to the next level is to let people see your work.

By providing a "tour environment" at FastCap we were essentially communicating to our people that they were doing an exceptional job, because people from all over the world were beginning to tour our facilities. We've even had dignitaries and high-level politicians come through to see what we're doing. Why? Because we are delivering exceptional results. At FastCap, we have never laid anyone off, nor cut salaries or pay rates, and, in spite of the biggest economic downturn in the last one hundred years, we continue to expand our business. We do business in forty countries and counting. We are a highly profitable company with the highest paid employees in our region from top to bottom. We have a lot to be proud of, and sometimes in our quest for continuous improvement, we lose sight of that.

Dino Rossi, Washington State, State Senator

Our success is due to a focus on building a culture of growing people. We don't just talk about it, we spend thousands of dollars every day training and teaching our people. This is known as "putting the

Rob McKenna, Washington State Attorney General

money where your mouth is!" People who tour our plant ask, "What do you do for new employee orientation?" Our response is, "Every employee is oriented every day they come to work." Most companies dust off the new employee manual and review it for a week or two and then 90% of it is forgotten. At FastCap we review our 13 goals, 20 principles, endless improvements, hundreds of products, every mistake, every raving customer response we receive, history, culture and the constitution every day. We've built that culture by investing time and money into training and teaching our people the value and rewards of improvement, going right back to what the VP of Lexus told me was the most important thing for any world class, premier company – teaching and training people.

At the end of the day, each one of us has the job title of process engineer. Our job is not to build products, but to improve the process of how we build our products. This is what makes us a distinctively Lean culture. The order of these improvements is equally important.

First we improve:

- The individual
- The process
- The product

It's double 'I'-PP (I.I.P.P).

We like to say at FastCap that we're in the business of growing people. The result of growing people is that we produce outstanding products; we work in an innovative environment where ideas are welcomed with the same enthusiasm whether they come from the entry-level employee or the CFO. The

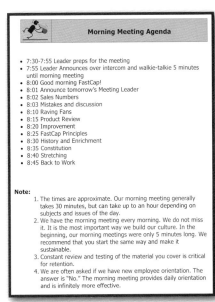

Morning Meeting Agenda

- 7:30-7:55 Leader preps for the meeting
- 7:55 Leader Announces over intercom and walkie-talkie 5 minutes until morning meeting
- 8:00 Good morning FastCap!
- 8:01 Announce tomorrow's Meeting Leader
- 8:02 Sales Numbers
- 8:03 Mistakes and discussion
- 8:10 Raving Fans
- 8:15 Product Review
- 8:20 Improvement
- 8:25 FastCap Principles
- 8:30 History and Enrichment
- 8:35 Constitution
- 8:40 Stretching
- 8:45 Back to Work

Note:

1. The times are approximate. Our morning meeting generally takes 30 minutes, but can take up to an hour depending on subjects and issues of the day.
2. We have the morning meeting every morning. We do not miss it. It is the most important way we build our culture. In the beginning, our morning meetings were only 5 minutes long. We recommend that you start the same way and make it sustainable.
3. Constant review and testing of the material you cover is critical for retention.
4. We are often asked if we have new employee orientation. The answer is "No." The morning meeting provides daily orientation and is infinitely more effective.

FastCap's Daily Morning Meeting Agenda.

At FastCap we have the best trained people in the world and we do it every day.

expectation of every person at FastCap is that things will continue to get better every day; the culture supports and demands it!

This is how you measure your progress of building a Lean culture: smiles. You will see more smiles because it feels good when everybody is experiencing improvement and working in a clean environment.

The number one thing that people want in life is to feel that their ideas matter and they are making a difference.

Nurturing people to be their best, taking the time to review results, listening to ideas for improvement and learning together is what our morning meeting is about. From the entry-level employee on their very first day of work all the way up to me as owner – we take on the process of learning and improving together. Nobody is given a pass and nobody is left out of the expectation for improvement. That's how we started building a culture at FastCap. The morning meeting was just the beginning.

> ## THE ONE THING:
> SHOW ME YOUR CHECKBOOK AND WHERE YOU SPEND YOUR MONEY AND I WILL SHOW YOU WHAT YOU VALUE.

Lean Works for You

Begin by outlining what your first morning meeting will look like. 5 minutes is all it takes to get started:

1. _____

2. _____

3. _____

4. _____

Make it easy and go to:
www.fastcap.com
Download the FastCap Morning Meeting Word document. Change it 99% or 1%, it's there as a FREE resource to get you going on your Lean Journey.

Lean resources:

1. Morning Meeting document.
http://bit.ly/wPwgQL

Chapter 9

Beyond the Morning Meeting

The morning meeting allowed us to implement the first stage of building a culture, which is teaching and training people. But we still needed to impart an expectation of continuous improvement. We needed people to make improvements on a daily basis so that we could produce a higher quality product at a lower cost, while also enjoying a regular sense of accomplishment in our work environment. Lean is not just about growing people so that they feel all happy and involved. It is also about results – measurable, concrete results, that show a continual pattern of improvement.

How did we do that? If I told my people, "Hey, I want you to make one improvement a day," they would look at me kind of cross-eyed. Most would respond, "I don't know if I can think of one improvement today." It sure sounds like a tall order, doesn't it?

So, I changed it again to something so simple. Remember the Hoks model? The beauty of their company was that they kept their process very simple in order to ensure the maximum "buy-in" from their people.

I said to my people, "Just give me a single 2 second improvement a day. That's it. That's all I ask for. A 2 second improvement."

There is not a person on earth, let alone a mouse or a hamster that can't figure out how to improve something by just 2 seconds. I made the bar so low that everybody could jump it, and indeed, that's what happened. I began with

Boys! The boss wants a 2 second improvement a day. We can do it!

the simple expectation of a 2 second improvement a day, but in order for me to make sure that people understood how they could possibly find a 2 second improvement every day, we came up with the next phase of building a culture of continuous improvement – the morning improvement walk.

Everyone reports to work at 7 o'clock in the morning. Our morning meeting goes from 8:00-8:30. Technically speaking, my people don't really work at their specific jobs from 7 to 8. Instead, we reserve that

Everyone in improvement mode from 7-8.

Showing a KanBan system improvement.

The stamp licker has a home now.

Get over here and look at my improvement.

Shadow foaming all the tools.

time for the 3Ss. Remember those? Our 3Ss are: sweep, sort and standardize. Sweep (clean their area), sort everything and remove anything that is ancillary and not necessary to their specific job and then standardize everything. By committing that first hour to the 3Ss, every person is given the opportunity to find a 2 second improvement. Sorting through the clutter that tends to build up in our work areas will always yield some kind of improved efficiency. Everyone knows they have at the very least one hour, from 7 to 8 am to make one small improvement in their own area of influence or workspace. In order to reinforce this idea, I began walking the shop floor every morning from department to department, greeting people saying, "Hi, Austin! What's your improvement for today?" or "What are you working on?"

When people tour FastCap they say things like "this is the cleanest place I have ever seen, you guys are fanatical, the salt and pepper is even labeled and shadowed on the lunch table."

Our second step toward building a Lean culture was a very simple process that absolutely everybody could buy into and participate in. We kept it simple enough and made sure to build it into the workday. There's not a place in the world that can't benefit from a 2 second improvement.

Recently I taught this 2 second improvement process to the staff at city hall, close to where I live. The first week everybody came up with improvements and some of the improvements saved them hours a day. Imagine that! I was only asking for 2 seconds, but people were delivering hours of improvements. This is the magic of making it simple.

When I explained the 2 second improvement to Harry Kenworthy, a consultant that I interviewed on my radio show, "The American Innovator," I asked him if he thought it sounded like something that would work in any environment.

Guys, this is not what I meant by "Growing People"... Now where is the improvement?

He said, "Absolutely." I said, "Well, why do you believe it worked so well at FastCap?" He said, "Simple, Paul. In order to make something stick, you must first:
• Set the expectation
• Inspect the expectation
• Reinforce the expectation

I didn't understand those three concepts from a business theory perspective, and I had not laid out the process with those steps in mind, but I was performing them without even knowing it. I expect my people to make a 2 second improvement, the expectation is made clear by building time into their work

Yuriy puts clear tape over the labels so that they hold up to continuous use.

day to make it happen. The morning improvement walk reinforced the expectation as I walked around. From time to time I find someone who is just "stuck" and I often assist them in finding a two second improvement. Finally, I reinforce that behavior by celebrating those improvements in the morning meeting.

The team leaders walk around and let our people demonstrate the different improvements that they've made in their area. It has been a very effective culture-building technique.

We've taken a further step to celebrate the really great ideas by videotaping them to play during the morning meeting. Before

Watching improvement videos in the morning meeting.

we did the videotaping, we would actually take the entire company to see different improvements. That became a logistical problem because we had so many people to walk around and it took too long. Also, the areas we were observing were generally small manufacturing cells and only the people in the front could see and hear the demonstrations.

When we decided to start cataloging the ideas on a video camera, we enjoyed four surprise benefits. The first was that we didn't have to drag the entire company around from department to department like a herd of cattle. The second benefit was that everybody could clearly see and hear the demonstration by watching the video at the morning meeting. The third – unexpected – benefit was that it began to sharpen the presentation and speaking skills of our people. It allowed them to develop their abilities to articulate their ideas and express themselves on camera, which is just a fantastic skill to have in this day and age. The fourth benefit is that we developed a powerful video library for teaching others what Lean improvements look like.

The cataloging and videotaping of our improvements also provided excellent promotional material. People who toured our facility could access these ideas for themselves by simply going to our website. This feature has become a teaching tool for the outside, and again, our own people are deeply gratified by the fact that people from all over the world are viewing their improvements and learning from them. My personal BHAG (big hairy audacious goal) is to change the world, and as you can see, my people are doing just that.

The morning improvement walk became the second important aspect of building a culture of continuous improvement, and it has yielded many more improvements than we ever even expected. That is the nature of Lean thinking though. Its benefits keep on giving. Now I know you must be wondering, "Paul, you do this every day?" The answer is YES! We have been doing this every day for over five years. We don't miss it. It's part of our culture. It's more important than building widgets or woodworking tools or anything else we do, because we know if we have world class problem solvers, it doesn't matter what we are building today or five years from now. We will have the capacity to do an excellent job at whatever is put in front of us.

The biggest problem people have with the idea of letting their people come up with a 2 second improvement is trusting they won't screw something up, or make the process worse. The answer is they will. They will make mistakes and become better problem solvers in the process. In order to do Lean correctly, you must trust that the system will produce the desired outcome. Even if you hit a pothole (or rabbit) along the way, the number one way people learn is by making mistakes. If you rob your culture of this experience you will rob yourself of the boundless innovations that could await you. Remember, we are looking for small improvements, so the mistakes should be small as well. Each mistake and each improvement will become a valuable part of building a culture of continuous improvement.

THE ONE THING:
TWO SECONDS WILL CHANGE THE WORLD!

Lean Works for You

Write down your first ten 2 second improvements:
(Remember the best place to start is with what bugs you.)

1. _____
2. _____
3. _____
4. _____
5. _____
6. _____
7. _____
8. _____
9. _____
10. _____

Lean videos:

1. Lean Morning Improvement Walk
http://youtu.be/3OEePS7Oh_g

2. Lean Dust Control
http://youtu.be/Su_c2UhSRDw

Chapter 10

Let's Do It in the Bathroom

At FastCap we have a lot of fun. One of the funniest things we do happens during the morning tours we give for visitors. After they have a chance to see our company in action, during the morning meeting and improvement walk, people always ask, "How do I get started? It seems so overwhelming."

That's when I say, "Oh, it's really quite simple," and then I lead them to one of our five bathrooms. I open the door and say, "Walk in here and I will show you how you begin to build a culture of continuous improvement."

They look at me like I'm crazy and respond with, "Are you serious? Really? You want me to learn how to do this by walking in your bathroom?" I say, proudly, "We have the cleanest bathrooms in the world. All of our bathrooms are identical, because our bathroom is the standard for what we think Lean should look like in the rest of our facility."

Come on in! Lean begins in the bathroom!

We created a standard that was easy for everyone to understand. After all, the bathroom is one experience that unites all of us and most of us will see it at least three or four times a day during our working hours. When we say that everything should look like the bathroom, people know exactly what we are talking about. Now, let me tell you what our bathroom looks like.

This book is full of pictures, as a way of giving proof of our Extreme Lean ways! You can see in the pictures that each bathroom has a stainless steel rack in it with all the supplies necessary – toilet plunger,

Every bathroom is standardized with the same cleaning supplies in the same places... It is very easy to maintain a spotless bathroom!

toilet bowl scrubber, paper towels, Windex™, wipes, a mop, aspirin, saline rinse, basically everything we use on a daily basis to maintain our bathrooms and keep them clean.

Clean toilet and the seat is DOWN!

Bathroom Cleaning Chart

When we first began the transformation of our bathrooms, one thing we noticed was that we had several different kinds of cleaners and methodologies to get the bathroom clean. It was not a standardized process. Some people liked Windex, some people liked 409™. We had a whole variety of different kinds of cleaners and processes to clean the bathroom, which is absolutely the antithesis of Lean. Remember the 3Ss we learned from Hoks – sweep, sort, and standardize? Keeping track of everybody's favorite cleaner is craziness and adds too much complexity to a task that should be straightforward. Now, everything is standardized.

On the door of every bathroom is a plastic laminated card that has pictures of the six steps necessary to clean the bathroom and a picture of the person who is responsible for cleaning it that day. At FastCap we don't have janitors. We all clean the bathrooms, including me.

The bathrooms stay perfect all day long, because a consequential component of Lean is respect for people. Leaving the bathroom cleaner than you found it is a very basic sign of respect and courtesy for others. The toilet seat is down, there is no pee on the toilet, no water spots on the mirror, and the sink is clean.

This is the way every one of our bathrooms are left all day long. I promise you, I am not exaggerating! You can walk in any one of our bathrooms at any time of day, and they will look identical to what they looked like in the morning when they were first cleaned. The reason is because there are three principles in play.

Number one (pun intended), leave everything better than you found it. If that's the case, everything is continuously improving.

Number two (sorry, I couldn't help myself), respect for people. Simple things like leaving the toilet seat down is a basic courtesies that shows respect for others. When you leave everything better than you found it, you are naturally cleaning up after yourself, and therefore, making things better for others, which is a sign of respect for others. Number three, create a standard that is accessible to everyone. We created our standard using a very basic model that everybody can relate to: the bathroom. The bathroom is visual and easy to understand. What better place to begin building a culture of continuous improvement than the bathroom?

1. Leave it better than you found it.
2. Respect for people
3. Create a standard

My advice for people wanting to create a Lean culture is to start in the bathroom and roll it out slowly from there. Go ahead, do it in the bathroom!

Building a Lean culture requires standardizing and simplifying everything. We settled on Windex™ (because I am Greek and all Greeks know that Windex will heal and clean anything. If you don't understand this joke watch *My Big Fat Greek Wedding* for an explanation). It's a running joke at FastCap; if all else fails, get out the Windex. Paul loves Windex. So

Windex is great for everything!

we use Windex on our bathroom counters, we use Windex on our floors, and on our lunch tables. We use Windex on the countertop. We have one cleaner that does a great job for just about every surface. This is just one example of why the bathroom has been created as an excellent model of how to standardize and simplify.

Back to the 3Ss, it's swept and kept clean in a very simple way. It's sorted – we got rid of all the ancillary products – and it's standardized. We use the same product in all bathrooms and the same checklist. As a matter of fact, everybody cleans a different bathroom every week. It rotates around and they can perform the task perfectly, because everything is in the same place, no matter where you go and that's 100% predictable. We made the process the expert, not the people. By doing so we free up all of our RAM memory for higher level thinking, for activities such as continuous improvement and innovation. We do not clutter our minds and waste our time searching for mundane items like cleaning supplies and plungers. If you don't know how to start thinking Lean, start doing it in the bathroom!

> # THE ONE THING:
> ## LEAN STARTS IN THE BATHROOM.

Lean videos:

1. Lean Bathroom
http://youtu.be/cul_Ypj0lnw

Chapter 11

How Do I Start?

Some of you, no doubt, are disappointed. Surely the world class business theory of Lean manufacturing taught in MBA programs and premiere business schools all around the world cannot be reduced to something this fun, simple and easy to implement. I've shared with you how Lean has rescued companies from the brink of bankruptcy and transformed them into multi-million dollar profit-making engines. I have also told you of companies like mine that were incredibly successful before implementing Lean and had all the trappings of greatness and still Lean has had a transforming effect on our performance and people. Now I am asking you to consider Lean thinking not only in your business pursuits, but also in your personal life. My team members tell stories of how they have used Lean principles to interact

Using your head, not your wallet. This simple improvement uses a string attached to a home-made wood pedal, and a pair of pliers as a crimping tool. The operator's hands are now free and so is his mind to think of the next great improvement.

with their children's teachers, real estate brokers and all types of contacts they encounter in daily life. Instead of the traditional shame and blame mentality, our people naturally ask, "How can I improve this?" "How can I do this better?" Average people are not used to this level of positivity, and Lean thinkers are positive, action-oriented people. Lean thinkers drill down and do not accept the standard answer of "No, I don't think we can do that;" instead we must improve the process and find a better way.

Let me assure you, if implementing Lean were a complicated process then I would not be writing this book. I'm an energetic entrepreneur with very little patience for academic exercises, technical instructions or any kind of a plan that requires tedious micro-managing. My goal is to get the word out to as many people as possible and watch the wave of improvement take over our companies, our communities and our relationships at home. Your business and your personal life can radically improve – becoming better than ever – by putting into action the simple, universal desire for continuous improvement.

The secret of world-class corporations like Toyota, New Balance™, and FastCap is that they do a few things so well that nobody can catch them. It's kind of like Irving Berlin's famous story about *The Hedgehog and the Fox*. The fox is very clever and can do a lot of things effectively, but the hedgehog knows how to do just a few things really well. The consistency of the hedgehog enables him to outfox the fox, day after day. That's the beauty of Lean. It's simple.

How do you get started? First, I am going to ask you to do a little research to familiarize yourself with what a Lean company *looks*

I'll take my daily 2 second improvement anyday over the craftiness of your plan. Catch me if you can.

Click on the video tab, then Lean videos on our FastCap website. They are all FREE!

like. We have an incredible website at www.fastcap. com. Click on the video tab on the home screen and you will find videos on everything I've talked about: the history of our company, the morning improvement walk, the morning meeting and my favorite the Lean desk. Start watching the videos. Soak in the energy we enjoy at FastCap.

The second thing you need to do is to take a tour. We have made every attempt at making the tour as available as possible through our website (thus making it as Lean as possible), but there are major benefits to an in-person tour. If it is at all possible, take the time and effort to visit a Lean company. To get a sense of the authenticity and power of a Lean culture, there is just no substitute for the flesh and blood interaction with the people on-site. Some of my favorites are Kaas Tailored (run by my friend Jeff Kaas)

Learn to see Lean tour at FastCap.

in Everett, Washington and Karl Wadensten's company, VIBCO in Providence, Rhode Island. If you are in Bellingham, Washington we invite you to visit us at FastCap. If you can't get to Japan, you might as well visit Toyota™ here in the USA at their plant in Lexington, KY. They have a fabulous tour that is really nothing short of breathtaking.

There are thousands of companies all over the world that can provide these tours for you, because integral to Lean culture is the desire to "pay it forward." Once you begin enjoying the fruits of a Lean culture, you just naturally want to promote it to others. That's how good it is and that's how you can measure if you're "getting it." It will always bring a sense of enthusiasm and excitement. People like feeling better about themselves and they are jazzed when they start getting more accomplished with less effort.

The third thing to do is to implement the morning meeting at your workplace. This begins the process of including everyone on the journey. Morning meetings are

Morning meetings build the culture!

about setting the expectation of continuous improvement, beginning with simply asking for a two second improvement from everyone. The first task for improvement will be the bathroom – did you think I was kidding? The bathroom is an easy first step that is visual and everyone has to use it at least three times a day.

The very next day after your first morning meeting, start with the morning walk to see how everybody is contributing to the process of improvement.

After you have been at this for about a year and you feel comfortable with the morning meeting and improvement walk, and after you have created a Lean bathroom, then the next thing you need to consider is teaching Lean.

Open up your facility, find out about other Lean thinkers in your

The more you teach Lean the better you are at being Lean.

Everyone in the facility teaches, not just management.

community and encourage visiting one another. When you begin to open your business for others to visit, you will begin to learn how to implement Lean in a whole new way. Why? Because when your people receive visitors who are interested in what they are doing, they take a renewed sense of pride in their work. That's the first benefit. When you teach things, you generally have to get a lot better at them. That's the second benefit.

The third benefit is that it's the right thing to do. Helping others and giving back is more important than making money; being purpose driven is more powerful than being profit driven. You will find that the most successful companies in the world have balanced the art of making money with the gift of sharing and helping others. That ethic of "paying it forward" is fundamental to becoming a Lean thinker.

So go ahead, take the plunge and become a Lean leader.

THE ONE THING:
START SMALL, DREAM BIG

Lean videos:

1. Lean in a Nutshell PDF document
http://bit.ly/pCOvvq

2. Lean Use Your Head Not Your Wallet
http://youtu.be/OuVfDJhf0ew

Chapter 12

Extreme Lean

There is nothing casual about a successful Lean culture; the commitment needs to be 1000%. When this drive for continuous improvement takes an emotional hold of the leadership, I've heard it described as Extreme Lean. Extreme Lean is when the leadership of an organization is <u>consumed</u> with eliminating waste through continuous improvement. "We are at war with waste," says Karl Wadensten. It is an emotional and gut level connection with the desire to see anything and everything with an eye toward simplifying, improving and eliminating waste.

I snapped this picture after 3 people left this mess on the table without cleaning up after themselves. My first thought was "Those pigs! How can anyone be so disrespectful?" My second thought was two bottles of water, a coffee, an espresso and scone generated an enormous amount of waste! As a Lean thinker I couldn't help but ask myself, "How can this level of waste be stopped?" I was emotionally engaged by the astounding amount of waste.

We are at war with waste!

Recently I visited a facility that had been practicing Lean for three years and the culture felt flat; there was no excitement. I learned that the executives only decided to try Lean because their competitors were practicing Lean. So, these executives tossed the concept to their mid-level managers and said, "Do this Lean thing." They basically washed their hands of any responsibility for how to implement Lean principles. They were only committed to Lean in regards to how it would support the bottom line, and as a result they had a flat, uninspiring culture. Sure, they were making improvements and we saw examples of 3S-ing, but it was vastly different from the passion I've seen in Japanese companies and a select few in the USA.

As a leader you must be fully engaged with your people in the process, otherwise Lean will look like the flavor of the month, just another business tool to be pushed aside when management returns home from the next business conference. Most leaders do Lean because they think it will make them more money. Only 2% of Lean leaders create dynamic Lean cultures by focusing on growing people, and not the bottom line. Extreme Lean is felt in the heart and the head.

If you are Japanese you can't be stressed; the Chinese are two days away by boat.

A great example of Extreme Lean is a Japanese company called Molten™. As we toured their facility, the President showed us a particular manufacturing cell where they were obsessing over eliminating 1/6th of a second in a one-minute process. I stood there with my jaw open realizing just how sloppy I was in implementing Lean. These people chased waste like my dog chases a cat. When I asked the President if he was stressed, he replied, "If you are Japanese, you do not know this word. The Chinese are two days away from us by boat and two weeks from the USA. If we don't chase waste with this level of passion, we will not have jobs."

The President of Hoks says emphatically, "These are the only vending machines in Japan on wheels! Yes, it seems crazy, but we can move them easily, clean behind them with no effort and it clearly conveys our passion to flexibility in the workplace."

Where did I get this intensity about becoming Lean? It started at the Hoks plant in Japan. When I saw what that company accomplished against all odds, something in my gut tripped like a wire going live. I immediately knew, "I want this for FastCap." The spirit and energy of the place inspired me to imagine my company going to levels I never thought possible. Since that experience my commitment to following through and helping others to see the power of Lean has never wavered, not even once. Remember, the Hoks tour happened after I had languished in Lean limbo for five years, and was looking for why I couldn't get Lean to take on a life of its own. If you are not passionate about

Hoks is so passionate about eliminating waste that they label every thermostat, wall switch and outlet. There is no time to waste on guessing. We are competing with the Chinese who pay their people 17 times less than ours.

improvement, then you need to keep studying, watching and learning and trying the baby steps until your wire gets tripped.

At FastCap we had one employee who was harder to convert to Lean thinking than most. One morning he was particularly frustrated with all the time we spent on our morning meeting and the improvement walk.

"Paul," he said to me, "we can't afford to spend all this time improving. We have too much work to do and we'll never get it done." I said, "We are an extremely successful company. Do you know why? Continuous improvement. Your job is not to produce Fastcaps, but to improve the process of how we produce Fastcaps, and your production concerns will take care of themselves."

One of my Lean teachers had a conversation with a Toyota executive about all the bad publicity from the lawsuits and allegations of stuck accelerators and faulty brakes. The executive did not resort to victim language, but simply lamented that some people in Toyota had become complacent with their success. They had lost their passion, their drive.

My sensei, Brad (of "Brad and Jon" fame from chapter 2) described the effect of a Lean culture as analogous to "wild mustangs." I swear his eyes were blazing wild when he described this! Wild mustangs, free from fear. They drive themselves from an instinctive, gut level, as though their lives depend on running. The full effect of creativity coming alive in people is as powerful as a herd of wild horses. The trick, of course, is keeping those horses running and free. There is never a time when it's ok to coast. That is "Extreme Lean."

A Lean culture is a free culture where people are trusted to express themselves and be creative... This is uncomfortable for most leaders.

Just before the economic crisis hit its full stride in 2008, I began to see troubling signs all around me. I saw companies that had been very successful and responsible in their financial dealings begin to teeter and crumble. As you know, FastCap is heavily dependent on construction and next to real estate and banking, you're hard pressed to find an industry that was harder hit by the recession. At this time we were doing well. We were in what I call "crazy Lean mode,"

Here I'm illustrating the difference between Lean and Waste. The box with the excessive wrapping is what most of our lives look like; the clean brown box I'm holding is what Lean thinkers are striving for – just what the customer needs and nothing more.

meaning we were riding high with company morale, great profits, international expansion and a very enthusiastic team of employees. Improvements were happening every day at all levels. Business took a downturn by 25%. Really good people and smart businessmen closed their doors. I decided that it was not the time to coast on our good fortune. If we wanted to escape the perils of the bad economy, we would need to stare it down and dare the recession to touch our shores. It was time to commit to full battle mode. It was time to go "Extreme Lean." This is called operating from a position of strength. Why should we wait for bad times to put on our battle dress?

I gathered my employees and began to brainstorm with them about our battle plan. We came up with three goals.

Goal 1: We will survive.
Goal 2: There will be no layoffs and no pay cuts.
Goal 3: Not only will we survive, but we will prosper through the recession.

The first action item was to scrap my dream expansion project. I

We stuck with our old facility and Leaned it out, used our heads and not our wallets and everyone kept their jobs.

I stopped my dream of building a new state of the art facility after years of planning and hard work. I then re-focused our team's energy into Leaning out our current older facility and it was the best decision I have ever made.

had set aside $5 million toward building a newer, bigger facility that would be a gleaming icon of our success. It was gut wrenching to give that up, but we all decided the money needed to stay in our hands as a reserve fund. There were too many land mines in the economy and any one of them could blow up on us. Saving money, not spending it, was the prudent thing to do. My friends and business associates could not believe I would stop this project midstream.

The next thing we did was to recognize that even with the 25% decline in business, we should cut our budget another 25%. We made all these cuts without touching salaries or jobs. We slashed our advertising and marketing budget in half from $500,000 to $250,000. Most companies do the opposite during bad times because conventional wisdom is that in order to stay afloat you have to spend a higher percentage of your income on promoting yourself and aggressively wooing customers. We cut spending in absolutely every department by 25%. No department felt picked on or singled out. We all carried the same burden. This is what Extreme Lean looks like. Even though we were already a model Lean company, we knew there was waste everywhere and we were determined to find it.

We were committed to carrying out our mission of continuous improvement on fewer resources in order to survive and prosper through the coming storm. Remember, we were already "Crazy Lean." Instead of going in with a spirit of resignation to face the bad economy, we charged forward, determined to improve and to do more with less – wild mustangs of creativity and innovation. Just as I have come to expect, our Lean determination paid off big. Something miraculous happened. Our business did not fold. It didn't even suffer. Every department found creative ways to cut spending while still finding improvements. My marketing

We went from a $5000 professional video camera to a $400 handheld camera and now we are successfully using the iPhone™ for hundreds of high-definition videos. At the same time we went from a 400 square foot video department full of equipment to a single computer workstation and now with the iPhone™ we film and edit, right where we stand, at the moment we are shooting. Now, that is one piece flow, just in time and no batch work. See how we make a Lean video on our website.

and advertising people created better, cheaper and more effective advertising campaigns. They accomplished more, with less money. Imagine that! From this experience came a favorite motto for our company: "Money suffocates creativity."

When money is no object we abdicate our most powerful resource: our ideas. It just gets too easy to throw money at problems and yet we see time and time again that money often creates problems rather than solving them. For example, it used to take us sometimes days to create a single video to post on the internet. We believed we needed to have all the right video equipment and a dedicated video room. That was one of the biggest wastes of money this company ever had. Today we can consistently produce videos with five separate scenes in under five minutes. This includes:

• Shooting the scenes
• Editing and trimming the scenes
• Inserting the scenes
• Applying the music track
• Adding titles and captions
• Starting the upload to YouTube™

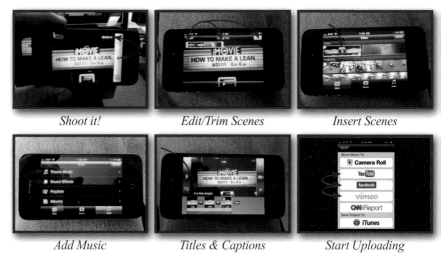

| *Shoot it!* | *Edit/Trim Scenes* | *Insert Scenes* |
| *Add Music* | *Titles & Captions* | *Start Uploading* |

If you want to see it happen, go to our Lean videos and watch "How to make a Lean video" and the review of the best cameras to get the job done. I would normally say it is so easy a child could do it, but kids are great at technology. Instead I will say it is so easy a 70-year-old with no technical experience could learn to do it in under five minutes. Since we think Lean, we have removed the barriers that typically hang people up and make the seemingly complex accessible to everyone. The real prize came when we actually met our third goal – to prosper. As a consequence of so many other businesses closing in the construction sector, high-end equipment became available at much lower prices. We were buying up equipment at half the market price, and sometimes even less than that, which enabled us to comfortably expand our business. As a result of our expansion, we hired more people and ended 2009 as one of our most successful years in business. During the most difficult economic downturn for our industry we actually had one of our most profitable years ever, with more jobs created, not less, and with excellent wages. That's the reward for going "Extreme Lean." We will weather anything that comes our way as long as we resist the temptation to become passive in our successes.

One of the many machines we bought for pennies on the dollar – creating 10 new jobs in the process.

> # THE ONE THING:
> WE ARE AT WAR WITH WASTE, A LITTLE ANGER AND PASSION AMONG THE SOLDIERS TOWARD THE ENEMY WON'T HURT A THING.

Lean videos:

1. Best Cameras
http://youtu.be/XD3E78f_leI

Chapter 13

Humble Lean

Besides having a 100% emotional commitment, a Lean leader must be humble. What does that look like? Let me give you a tangible goal. Commit yourself to validating, complimenting and/or recognizing the work of your employees at least ten times a day. Your people should be accustomed to hearing you say things like, "That's a great idea, Bob," or "Mary, I appreciate how hard you've worked on this project," or "Actually, John, I like your idea better than mine." When humility becomes a central attribute of the Lean leadership a vortex of creativity and buy-in will follow. When there is a culture where people know there is not an egomaniac in charge they can begin to grow and thrive. They know that leadership is singular in their focus to give others credit above themselves. There are no politics, no jealousies or rivalries because everybody knows they'll be acknowledged for their contribution and more importantly, they understand their job is to acknowledge others' contributions. A Lean culture is a generous environment. It's generous in giving credit to others, generous in respect, generous in offering ideas, support and help.

The Lean leader has an ego strong enough to solicit and welcome ideas from absolutely every person involved and will recognize everybody's contribution as valuable. In fact, a Lean leader gets excited by the prospect of unleashing all that untapped creativity and problem-solving genius that lies dormant in most organizations.

While many people will be shy and not so forthcoming at first, it is a universal human desire to be validated and respected. Once they get used to being asked, "What bugs you?"

Four things a Lean leader must say regularly to his people:
1. "Great job, I appreciate the work you are doing."
2. "Mary, Bob, that is a great idea!"
3. "Mary, Bob, I like your idea better than mine!"
4. "I'm wrong, you are right, I learned something."

An ocean wave of creativity awaits the organization that can be led humbly.

or "How would you fix this?" you can expect an ocean of creativity flowing through your organization in no time.

In an amazing coincidence, while writing this chapter, one of my employees, Pavlo, approached me on the shop floor. He noticed that I had submitted an order for the wrong material to use for one of our products. He said, "Paul, I was just wondering if you intended to order 'brand X', since we had discussed this other brand would probably be superior in performance." I slapped my forehead in recognition and said, "Oh, wow, thank you so much. You are absolutely right." I still had time to cancel the wrong order and change it to the correct material. I thanked Pavlo profusely for catching my mistake. Later that day, Pavlo, who is 6'3" and a specimen of athletic perfection and should have an ego the size of Texas, made a point of approaching me to say, "Paul, I thought you should know that it was actually Alexey who caught that mistake. He just had to leave early, so I told him I would pass it on. I just wanted to make sure you knew that."

This is the spirit of a Lean culture. When the leader is willing to be corrected and has no ego issues with sharing credit, that same generous and supportive spirit flows between everybody. In a less hospitable environment, Pavlo might have grumbled about my mistake, shaking his head all the while watching the mistake lead to more mistakes and then after all that wasted energy might have been satisfied saying, "See? I knew it wouldn't work." Instead, he felt completely comfortable raising his concern with me. Also, Pavlo could have accepted my gratitude, happy to take credit, but instead he graciously gave credit where credit belonged – with another employee, Alexey.

Another effect of humble leadership is that it builds a culture that frees people from anxiety or reluctance in sharing their ideas. Rejection is not an issue because it's perfectly acceptable to throw out a suggestion for improvement and then realize maybe it's not such a great idea after all. Nobody's feelings are hurt and nobody feels the pressure to be right all the time. We can make ourselves a bit vulnerable that way because we are strong and united in our desire to continuously improve with a focus on improving the life of the customer.

Not too long ago a team of engineers and business managers from Bombardier, the people who make Learjets, recently toured FastCap. One of them shared a story with me. He had attended a retirement party for an engineer friend. After the engineer had received so many gifts and well wishes, he reflected for a moment on his 30-year career at his company. With some regret he said, "For thirty years they had the work of my hands. They could have had the work of my head and heart for no extra cost, but they never asked."

Lean leaders will draw out the gifts and skills of the whole person. This is what I heard so loud and clear from the Lexus Vice President in Japan so many years ago. "The most important thing is our people. We don't care about the next technology, the next sales strategy or the next great model. We invest in our people."

And finally, you will draw out the best your people have to offer if you approach them with humility and gratitude. Lean leaders must respect their people and recognize that each person brings their own unique genius to the table. If you think about it, this takes a lot of pressure off you as a leader. What a relief that you don't have to come up with every good idea! You have an ocean of possibilities and ideas just waiting to be tapped into from your people. Why would you ignore or put on the shelf your most valuable source of genius?

Lean leadership yields the best possible products and services because it unleashes the best that every employee has to offer, without jealousy, without territorial rivalry and without retribution. Someone once told me politics is the 9th waste and it's a big one that is mostly ego driven. Only someone with a strong sense of self can be a Lean leader, because being humble is a sign of authenticity and generosity.

In the end, this book is really not about Lean or operational excellence, 2 second improvements, a culture, 3S-ing or Learn to See tours. It is all about Leadership excellence. When leaders lead with world class principles that are thoughtfully applied, the sky is the limit.

> ## THE ONE THING:
> ### HUMILITY IS THE PATH
> ### TO GREATNESS.

Lean videos:

1. 2 Second Lean Improvement
http://youtu.be/6qhE4WicKoI

2. Lean Lantech,
Excellence in Leadership
http://youtu.be/fOotGdcDQ8o

Chapter 14

The Three Pillars of Lean

Just over a year ago, I made the decision to write *2 Second Lean*. I did so for a couple of reasons.

First, people were curious. They would visit FastCap, see our Lean culture in living color and want more information on how to build such an unusual culture. It made a lot of sense to put my thoughts on paper and tell our story. I wanted to share our journey— and the details of how we implemented Lean—in order to be more effective in helping other people.

On tour at FastCap

The second reason was to express my ideas more succinctly on paper and provide a "clear process" which is at the heart of Lean thinking.

It is now one year later and I have a lot of thoughts about what has transpired— and the content of the book. One thing is for sure—the book has been popular! People like it. It's simple, it's short and it makes the concept of Lean accessible to everyone. I wanted everybody— whether they have a Ph.D. or are just beginning a career as an 18-year-old—to be able to understand, implement and build a Lean culture.

The Three Pillars of Lean

Paul on the hot seat

2 Second Lean gave me a lot of exposure. People began asking me to come speak to their organizations and their companies in different countries around the world. I began asking myself how I could improve the message of *2 Second Lean*. Lean is about planning, doing, checking, re-evaluating and improving everything endlessly. So, here we go... this is how I have improved the message of *2 Second Lean*.

I came up with *Paul's Three Pillars of Lean*. When I would go to the shop floor and see the problems people were wrestling with, it became very clear that I was missing something. In Lean circles, it's very common to say that two of the pillars of Lean are the elimination of waste and continuous improvement. I disagree. Lean is getting people to **see waste**. Seeing waste is the first pillar of Lean. If you can't identify the eight wastes in everything you do, then it's very difficult to eliminate the waste. The first pillar of Lean is to teach your people to **see waste**!

If you're going to build a Lean culture, you need to look at every process and ask the question, "Bob, what are the eight wastes and which ones can you see in the process you are doing right now?"

First, make sure that all your team members **know the eight wastes** like they know their own birthday. Teaching the eight wastes is not achieved with a handout, email, or seminar. You need to teach the eight wastes every single day! At FastCap, we simply review the eight wastes every day in our morning meeting. Every morning one person has to hold up their fingers and go over the eight wastes, and they have to tell a story that illustrates all the wastes.

8 Deadly Sins of Waste

1. **Over-production.** *Make the 8 wastes relevant and fun.* The number one waste is <u>over-production</u>. It is the "mama muda," present in all the other wastes.
2. **Transportation.** We transport the <u>over-produced</u> goods.
3. **Excess Inventory.** Then we put those <u>over-produced</u> goods in inventory.
4. **Defects.** Then we have defects and we have to rework those <u>over-produced</u> goods.
5. **Over-processing.** Then we have over-processing as we rework defects in the <u>over-produced</u> goods.
6. **Wasted Motion.** Then we have to handle those <u>over-produced</u> goods. So we have wasted motion.
7. **Waiting Time.** Then we have to force our customers to wait as we rework the defects in the <u>over-produced</u> goods.
8. **Wasted Potential.** Then we have wasted employee potential, because our team members are reworking waste instead of focusing on seeing waste, eliminating waste and letting value flow to the customer.

<u>The First Pillar</u>

As I said, every morning one of our fifty-two team members holds up eight fingers and tells us the story of waste. It is so deeply ingrained in our team members that when waste exists in a process that they're doing, it is very easy for them to see. The first and most important thing that I've learned is what I call the First Pillar of Lean: people must **see waste**.

Learning to see waste

The Second Pillar

The second pillar is that every person must continuously improve everything. The essence of the book *2 Second Lean* is making small incremental improvements that quickly accumulate into a significant body of work. A year later I'm 100% behind that concept, even more than ever, because it flat out works—and it's so simple. So first, you see the waste and second, you **continuously improve everything, everybody, every day**.

The Third Pillar

Now, the meat of my revisions to the book is related to the first and third pillars. The first pillar—people must see waste—was a twist or clarification to what most people regard as an important pillar of Lean thinking. The second pillar—make small continuous improvements to everything!

The third pillar is probably the most exceptional of all. This pillar is something that frankly caught me off guard. I just didn't realize why we were so successful in building a Lean culture. The Third Pillar of Lean is...you must **make "before and after" videos of all your improvements**. You must show the work area and the process before and after. I know you're saying, "What does that have to do with Lean, Paul?"

Everything! When you are developing a culture, you want to document the development of that culture. Do it in a fun way so that people will enjoy watching and want to join in the party. This adds an enormous amount of fresh emotional energy. What I tell people to do is just take your iPhone, your smartphone, your point-and-shoot—I don't care what it is, but do not go out and buy a professional movie camera—and record with the camera that is in your pocket. Do not go out and buy professional editing software; it is not necessary. All you need is simply a phone and an app like iMovie for editing the video right on your phone. **Keep it simple and get it done**.

Keep it simple - use your phone, not a video camera

iMovie app for editing

The best example I can give of making this concept work is how the amazing team at Walters & Wolf did it with one of their first videos called "Hauling the Mail." It is simple, funny, low tech and culture building. This video has it all and Walters & Wolf is on Lean fire!

Want to know a secret? I first started making videos about four years ago, but it took me two years to make my first video! In other words, I should have been making videos six years ago, but I got paralyzed because I wanted everything to be perfect. I bought all kinds of film gear and lighting and software, but I never made a video because I was waiting for everything to be perfect. Then I realized the folly of that. If you just do it, you'll learn so much "by just doing it." That is really the story of *2 Second Lean*. If you just make a small improvement, you'll learn so much that the next improvement will be that much better.

It's the same thing with videos. Just make it **now**—with the phone that is in your pocket. Make "before and after" videos **now**. Do not move a thing in your work area until you record in living color the chaos you are working in now. The video "Reforming Little Pigs" illustrates exactly what I am talking about. Do not change anything until you show the "before and after," because in doing so you clearly see the contrast and show your team the power of continuous improvement—and how to become a Lean thinker.

I began to instruct companies to do this and the results were phenomenal. It was literally like pouring gasoline on a bonfire. They made one video and they were able to show it to different branches and locations of their company. The next thing you know, they made another video. In just a few weeks, they made forty videos. I realized this was a critical component. It builds a library of success and a library for training all your current and future employees. This is a powerful concept.

One of the reasons why FastCap took off in terms of its Lean journey and why everyone was so interested in it, is that we documented what we were doing with our cheesy little videos—and everybody loved them. If it was good enough for us, why not instruct everybody to do it and make it a pillar for building a Lean culture? Indeed, that's what I've been telling people all over the world. The more I say it, the more people look at me and say, "Wow! I never thought about that; it makes perfect sense."

They begin to do it and the next thing that happens is that they begin to collaborate with us and send us their improvement videos. We post them on our website and it allows people all over the world to learn about the way other people are doing things. This is exciting news.

Lean improvement videos

One and a half years after publishing the book, my takeaway is *The Three Pillars of Lean*: First, see waste. Second, continuously improve everything, every day. Third, make "before and after" videos.

Still wondering about making videos? Let me tell you a story. Yesterday, I interviewed two ninth-graders, Natalie and Mikayla from Cornerstone Christian School. Their teacher Darryn Kleyn is doing a fantastic job of teaching the kids Lean concepts and building a Lean culture in his classroom. The kids are a nonstop-video-production machine. They are making so many videos on their lean improvements—and they are so good. Watch the "What is Lean?" video under the Lean Kids heading at fastcap.com.

Darryn and his lean class

I asked Natalie, "After one year of learning Lean, what is the one thing that could be improved upon to get the kids to better understand Lean?"

Mikayla & Natalie
What is lean?

She said, "Show more examples of Lean in action and use less words and theory." I rest my case...from the mouths of babes.

When I set out to write the book *2 Second Lean*, my goal was to explain how to build the Lean culture—and for everyone to do it in just one year instead of the eleven years it took me. I also wanted to share my many mistakes to save someone else from making the same ones. If I had known the information I know now, it would have been so simple to build a Lean culture. I know that I could step into any organization and implement these three simple pillars and make a significant impact in a short period of time.

THE ONE THING:
LEARN TO SEE WASTE.

Lean videos:

1. Three Pillars of Lean
http://youtu.be/R1e0wIyz9hY

2. Hauling the Mail
http://youtu.be/B2VemLCV8i0

3. Reforming Little Pigs
http://youtu.be/Lj6NsliY674

4. What is Lean?
by Natalie & Mikayla
http://youtu.be/BV0JMky36mE

5. Learning to See Waste
by Jaymie
http://youtu.be/EWAiD0v46vo

Chapter 15

Freaking Good Questions

One of the improvements I've made in my speaking engagements is the result of a suggestion from someone in the audience. In Lean speaks terminology this is "going to the shop floor." I have always been very comfortable with people interrupting me in the middle of my talk to ask questions, but the suggestion was to "allow fifteen minutes for people to ask questions at the end of every talk." I began

How can I improve?

to implement this new idea. It's worked so well that I decided to recap the top ten questions people ask me.

Some of them may be a little unusual, but all the more reason why it would be appropriate for me to answer them. I think a lot of people *think* these questions, but are afraid to *ask* them. I will start with the most unusual, but most common one.

Question 1 Paul, how do you feel about luxury?

Answer This is a very interesting question. I think it's asked because people see my desk and realize that I have no office and that I am such a minimalist in the way I conduct myself in my business.

I love luxury...this is my car!

They think, "Man, this guy must be opposed to luxury. He must be opposed to having anything nice."

I can assure you, nothing could be further from the truth. I am awash in luxury in my life. I can afford luxuries that most people can't, because I'm not wasting so much in the way I run my company. Lean is not an austerity program. Lean is eliminating non-value-added activity. We call that waste. If it's valuable for me to wear a beautiful Breitling watch, then that's not wasteful for me and I want Breitling to continue to make their artistic creations. If there is value in me flying my own plane around the world and it helps me do my job more effectively, then that is not wasteful. Lean is about eliminating non-value-added activity. A beautiful watch reminds me every second of the value of impeccable craftsmanship and attention to detail. My plane allows me to go anywhere at any time and gives me the value of total flexibility.

Lean is not an austerity program

There could be waste in how I maintain my plane, the way I fly my plane or the missions I fly with my plane—and that is open to scrutiny and improvement. However, the very act of having an airplane or a nice watch or a nice car, in and of itself, is not waste. As a customer I value the benefits these accoutrements bring. These luxuries are the result of me carefully managing my capital and I feel zero guilt over having them. Lean is not socialism. It is thoughtful capitalism.

Obviously, what you do with such accoutrements could have elements of waste. But, remember, that is open to scrutiny and improvement by the owner of the luxury—and no one else. Why do I say this? Because for all of us, rich or poor, we are awash in waste. Pointing fingers at someone else is not a kind thing to do and is definitely not as productive as solving your own problems. Luxury, in and of itself, is not waste. I love luxury. I have a lot of nice things and I can afford a lot of those things because I am a Lean thinker. I'm careful to see and eliminate waste at every corner.

Question 2   Do you have a high or low turnover?

Answer   We have a very low turnover. FastCap is a sought-after place to work, because it's a place where people feel validated. Their opinions and their ideas matter. In setting out to build a Lean culture, one of my objectives was to make the HR portion of our company much less burdensome. If we created a dynamic company, we would become a magnet for talent rather than having to search for talent.

Lean reduces employee turnover dramatically—to the point where it's almost nonexistent. Occasionally, we have an employee leave. Generally, it's only because they are going to school to pursue their dream of becoming a doctor, an attorney or a CPA. Turnover is extremely low, because we value human beings and we value their opinions.

Question 3   Do you ever get people that don't get it and don't want to cooperate?

Answer   Absolutely. In the beginning, at least fifty percent of the people that worked at FastCap either left or we fired them. Nowadays, it's very uncommon for us to have someone who doesn't get it. The reason is two-fold.

First, we are very deliberate in the way we hire people. We look for two characteristics—people who are humble and curious. We want people who don't act and feel like they know it all. We want people to be naturally curious about life. The minute we get somebody in an interview who tells us about everything they know and who is not really intrigued about what we're doing and the way we conduct ourselves as a company, we know that this person doesn't really possess the characteristics we need in our team members. We need humble, curious people. That's why we're so deliberate in the way we hire.

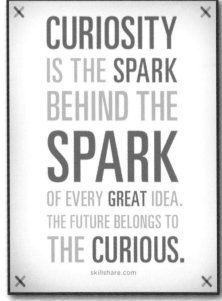

CURIOSITY IS THE SPARK BEHIND THE SPARK OF EVERY GREAT IDEA. THE FUTURE BELONGS TO THE CURIOUS.

skillshare.com

The second reason is that our culture is so strong—and positive—that it only takes a week or two for a person to absorb it. When you create a culture that's firm and consistent, then naturally, it's going to be very easy for people to understand your way of thinking. There will always be someone who doesn't want to get on board with the way you do business. In the beginning it was difficult. Now it is easy. One of my favorite sayings is, "Lean is hard work that makes everything easy." That is for sure. To better understand what our culture feels like through the eye of a young new employee, watch the interview with Hannah, a 16-year-old FastCap team member. Scan the QR code at the end of this chapter

Hannah

Question 4   Do you do Lean at home and what is your house like?

Answer   I love Lean. I improve everything I do everywhere I go. Whether I'm on vacation, at home, at work or flying my plane, I am constantly trying to refine processes, eliminate waste and make things easier. Most people are a little disconcerted by someone who is so fanatical about Lean, but I can assure you, Lean brings great joy to my life. I get so much more done than most people.

As a result of people asking me, "Do you do Lean at home?" I've made several videos showing people what my house looks like and how I've implemented Lean in my home. Here's a fun one to give you a glimpse... Lean at home.

The things that I do are so easy because I think Lean everywhere I go. My wife and I have just spent the entire weekend implementing Lean improvements in our closets. Today our closets are magical. My wife has a special closet that she uses for decorations for the house for different seasons. She has special decorations for the Fourth of July, spring, fall, Thanksgiving and Christmas. The house is always very festive and beautifully

Leanne's Lean closet

adorned.

The problem was that her decorations were not very well organized. So I asked, "How can we make this process better?"

I worked with my wife for two straight days and we made her the most amazing closet. All of her flower arrangements are precisely put away, her wreaths are hung beautifully and all the different candles are in separate bins. So now, when it's time to decorate our house, it's a simple process. My wife enjoys it and there's nothing burdensome about it.

Leanne's Lean closet

That's why Lean is so cool. Lean takes things that traditionally could be difficult or arduous and makes them simple and fun. And you have the added benefit of exercising your mind, because it becomes a big game about how to improve everything you do. The goal of Lean is to have zero struggle.

Question 5   What do you do about people who don't get it and don't buy into Lean in the way they do their work? Do you point out their waste?

Answer   This is perhaps one of my favorite questions to answer, because it is one of the most important answers to understand. You and I have enough waste in each of our lives to last us ten lifetimes. Do not look at anybody else's waste. Focus only on yours.

I made this point really clear recently in a tour at our company. Some people from another manufacturing company visited our facility. They were on the manufacturing side of the company. After the tour was over, one of the individuals said, "I want to know how we can implement Lean in the office."

I looked at him and asked, "Why? Are you in the office? I thought you said you were on the manufacturing floor."

He replied, "We are, but our office is so screwed up."

Then I said, "That is one of the biggest mistakes you'll ever make in your whole life. Focus on you. Focus on eliminating your waste. Believe me. You have enough for ten lifetimes."

When people see how much your area has improved, how much easier your work is, how much more they can depend on you, how consistent you are and how the quality of your product improves, they will want to know how you're doing it. Then you can show them. And then they will be eager to learn and begin their own Lean journey. But do not try to get your wife, your dog, your hamster, your cat or your co-workers to do Lean.

Focus on yourself. You and I have so much waste. This has been one

of the most critical points that I have learned in the last couple of years as I've talked to people and toured manufacturing plants and companies around the world. Focus, focus, focus on yourself.

Focus on yourself

Question 6   Do you give your employees incentives to improve?

Answer   In the beginning, we did and this was perhaps one of the biggest mistakes we made. We have since learned that Lean is our job. It is not something we do above and beyond our job. Continuous improvement is everyone's first and foremost job every day of their life. The first incentive for making Lean improvements is that life keeps getting better when you are thinking Lean!

When we gave monetary incentives, we felt that people were making the improvements because they wanted the

Can I entice you to do your job?

$5.00 or $10.00 incentive for every improvement they made. When we took the incentive away and said, "This is your job. Your job depends on it..." people realized that we were serious about Lean. We hired them because we wanted to use their brains, not just their hands. This is a game changer because most people don't feel like they're appreciated for what they contribute intellectually to the job. They feel that we just want them to build widgets.

We want your brain!

We changed the paradigm and said, "Your value is in your mind." When we did that, people got on board at an entirely different level. It is my humble opinion that paying people to do Lean is a mistake. Giving incentives takes the emphasis off of what the purpose of a company is.

The purpose of a company is to improve the quality of the customer's life. The purpose of a company is to deliver value at a very high level to the customer. The purpose of a company is to strip away the non-value-added activity and deliver to the customer more value consistently day after day, month after month, year after year. When you do that, your stature increases in the eye of your customer, your customer keeps coming back for more and then you make more money.

When you set the focus of each team member on making continuous improvements every day for the rest of their life, it changes the

Respect

paradigm. It takes the focus off of them and puts it back on the customer. It frees team members to focus on collaborating with other team members to deliver more value to the customer.

The second incentive for making Lean improvements is that they earn respect from the customer, their team members and from me. Every human being longs to be respected, but most people never get it.

Question 7 What if I don't want to be efficient in everything I do? I like walking around; I get more exercise.

Answer That is your prerogative. What you must understand is that Lean is hard work that makes everything easy. A little bit of effort can make your life experience a lot more enjoyable. When you couple the concept that "Lean is hard work that makes everything easy" with a global perspective, then you'll know why I pursue Lean in such an intense fashion.

I have come to learn that time is the great equalizer. Every human being gets 24 hours a day. We all get the same 24 hours—rich or poor, educated or uneducated. What we do in that 24 hours determines in large measure the success and happiness that we will enjoy in life. If you are a highly productive individual who is highly disciplined and reliable to your team members, your family and the other people you work with, it goes without saying that you will have a better life experience.

Time is the great equalizer.

If you're an unproductive person that doesn't get a lot done, is not reliable to your team members, your family and the other people you work with, then inevitably, there's going to be more disappointment and more friction in your life. Lean allows you to optimize and get more out of those 24 hours. When you get really good at Lean and very proficient at seeing waste, you will take 24 hours and seemingly get 48 hours out of them. I say this a little tongue-in-cheek, but when people come to our plant and see the way our people work, the smiles on their faces and the collaboration that exists among all of our team members, they're a little taken back by such a positive environment. My response is, "I would put my people up against anybody else in the world." Why? Because in just 8 hours, my people get done what most people get done in 40 hours.

People have a hard time believing we could be that much more productive. At Fastcap, work flows so naturally that people don't struggle to do their work; they enjoy their work. They have emotional energy when they do their work and the net result is significantly higher productivity. Again, you don't have to do Lean, but remember, time is the great equalizer. What you do with those 24 hours in large measure defines who you are and the happiness you enjoy each and every day of your life.

Question 8   Ashley, from the UK, asked, "Our workload has increased so much recently and we are struggling with the physical time to make the improvements, even when working overtime. It's hard to have a meeting every day and stand there and say, 'I know we had this problem yesterday, but we just haven't had the time to fix it.' My employees are really focusing on ways and coming up with some great improvement ideas, but the list of possible improvements is starting to back up because we don't have the time to implement them. Any thoughts?"

Answer   Sometimes it makes no sense to stop and do 3S'ing and improving when the workload is overwhelming. So I will answer the question by telling a story about what happened at FastCap.

Many years ago, we worked overtime regularly, and even on the weekends, because our workload was so great. We seemed to never be able to catch up. And then I said to everyone, "Stop. Stop working. We're going to clean our areas. We're going to 3S everything and we're going to make improvements. And if it takes us one hour or even four hours every day to do it, I don't care. We're going to do it and then we're going to work."

We meet & study daily ...and then we work.

Now, as you can imagine, there was great angst among all my employees, because they thought they would do nothing but get further and further behind. I assured them that if they took the time to improve and create an orderly, clean and well-organized work area, they would actually get more work done and they would catch up.

So we went ahead and made the commitment to 3S'ing and improving—regardless of the work load—and lo and behold, we caught up. Not only did we catch up, but we do millions of dollars more in business with a similar size crew and we never work overtime. That is the difference between making continuous improvement a priority and doing it when it is convenient. Improving first not only gives you the improvement, it lightens the load and allows you to keep up with accelerating demand.

It is counterintuitive and I understand this. But I've learned this lesson and I am 100 percent committed to it. We make sure that our work areas are 3S'd and that everyone has made a 2 second improvement before we ever begin our production work. When work flows, chaos is eliminated. Lean is not just a convenient belief; it is at the cornerstone of great companies. The more that Lean becomes a consuming priority, the faster work will flow—and improvements will pay the dividend of operational excellence.

Question 9   Another question from Ashley... "Motivation. When it's all just getting you down, and it's one of those days, how do you motivate yourself? Bear in mind this is early days for Lean for our company, so it isn't self-powered yet. My employees look to me for their motivation, so seeing me down has a negative effect. Any tips?"

Answer   Ashley, as always, you ask excellent questions. I'll be honest with you. I've had those moments. I have a very rich life and I don't mean just financially. I have a lot of joy and success in my life. I have a lot of good relationships with people around the world. And I credit all of that to the fact that I have chosen to follow historical principles of greatness. In other words, the choices that I have made in my life have been determined by principles that have produced great results throughout history.

These are principles that, when implemented by any human being throughout the course of time, have produced astounding results—

not good results—astounding results. The best example for me is the principle followed by our founding fathers—all men are created equal! The result is a country that has done more good for more people than any organized form of government in the history of man. Not perfect, far from it! But that single idea has become the touchstone for people from every nation. Millions are free today because of principles that produce great results.

Historical principles of greatness

My Favorite Principles

- Make people the center focus of your life. This is perhaps my favorite.
- Pursue the right thing over profit. The profit will follow.
- Teach and train. Any time you train an individual intensely, you dramatically enhance their ability to perform a job consistently—significantly more so than those people who are only moderately or occasionally trained.

The best example of teaching and training is the Navy Seals. When you take people that have been trained at such a high level and put them into stressful situations, they perform consistently 99 percent of the time. I ask myself, "If I take these principles and make them the centerpiece of the way I conduct myself, is it inevitable that I'm going to get a great result?"

U.S. Navy SEALS

So, on those days when I question, "Wow, do I really want to do this any more? This is a lot of work. Do people appreciate it? This is hard..." I always reflect back on the fact that I have done the hard thing. I have put my head down and just plowed forward by implementing these principles. That is why my life is full and rich. These ideas produce great result.

So, I am never going to deviate from following these principles. Historically they have produced sustainability, evenness, joy, satisfaction, and yes, profit. A focus on others brings me enjoyment and happiness. If I weren't focused on helping people, I wouldn't have the rich relationships that I have with people around the world. That keeps me motivated. What motivates me is a historical body of work that screams that these principles and ideas work. Don't give up!

Question 10   Sam from Israel asked... "I just watched your video about 'Making Lean Stick.' As always, I love the focus and simplicity of your message. But I was wondering about a hypothetical question. From what I understand from you and the book, the 2 Second Lean approach was developed a few years into your Lean journey. Do you think that if you had started with the three-step approach you reference in the video (teach people to see the waste, get them to fix what bugs them, and make before-and-after videos), you would have been able to come as far as you have?

Sam

"For example, in chapter two of your book, you describe how you guys got the setup time on your machine down from 45 minutes to 5 minutes. Do you think if you had started with the 2 Second Lean approach, you would have been able to do that?

"Or, in other words, how do you go from the 2 Second Lean concept, which seems to be more locally-focused, to solutions that affect the entire system from end-to-end? (It's possible that I don't understand the concept fully, so I may be misrepresenting it when I say it is locally-focused.)"

Answer   Sam makes an excellent point. With 2 Second Lean I seem to be focused on making small improvements and it appears that I am not a proponent of kaizen events. Yet, when Brad and John first came to our facility to teach us, they utilized kaizen events as the primary method to drive improvements.

First, you should know that the very reason we have such powerful results at FastCap is because of the 2 Second Lean approach. I promise there is more than meets the eye, or I have not done a good job of explaining all the behind-the-scene processes that are focused on the big picture, the entire value stream.

My focus with 2 Second Lean was to develop an easy strategy that would allow people to build a Lean culture and be successful in getting everyone on board. Over the last eleven years I have found that it is the small incremental improvements that do the best job and, in fact, do a better job than large kaizen events. Having said that, it doesn't mean that kaizen events don't have value; they just are not my preferred strategy.

Global Lean

I think of this as Global Lean, because at the end of the day, everybody has got to understand that what we're trying to do in any process, big or small, is take the waste out. We want to allow maximum value to flow to the customer. When you take the initial look at any process, it is important that you look at it globally.

You should not just focus on removing a small amount of waste from a particular step, because that step, in and of itself, might be waste. You could remove all the waste you want out of a process, but the bottom line is that the process itself might not deliver value to the customer. This would be a classic example of over processing.

Stand back and ask yourself, "What is it that we're trying to do for the customer here? What value are we trying to flow to the customer?"

First, look at it from this global perspective in conjunction with making small incremental improvements. I failed in my quest to make things simple by not giving proper attention to a global perspective. Our people have a global perspective, but I never discussed that and how we achieve that crucial component.

Every day we teach our team a series of principles that make up the core of our corporate philosophy. One of those principles is that Toyota never attempts to remove the waste out of any process unless they can cut it in half. At first glance, this principle does not seem to jive with the concept of 2 Second Lean, however, in reality, it dovetails perfectly.

Cut waste in half

Our team knows that the goal is to take a process that takes ten minutes and turn it into five minutes and then take the five minutes to two and a half minutes. They see the big picture and the brush that applies the paint is the 2 second improvement. The mechanics of how they're going to get there is done through small incremental improvements.

Our team also knows to look for the largest constraint. They have been trained to understand that the bottleneck—the biggest backup of work in a particular process—is the best place to see and eliminate waste.

They also know to ask themselves, "Is the activity that I'm doing delivering value to the customer—or is it just a process that's been added on? Am I trying to eliminate waste even though the process is delivering no value?" They understand these three concepts keenly. They understand that we don't want to do anything unless we're delivering value to the customer.

If we put a plastic bag around an item, is there any value for the customer? Sure it's nice to put a plastic bag around an item, but is there any value in it? If there's no value, we're not going to try to improve the process by reducing the size of the bag or finding a faster way to put the bag on. If the bag adds no value for the customer, it is waste.

A great example of this is the packaging of Apple products. Recently, I bought another iMac for our company. I was surprised when I opened the box. There was a minimal amount of packaging—less than the last time I bought one six months ago. I noticed that they didn't have a plastic bag around the computer. The computer was sandwiched between two pieces of foam with the power cord and a small manual enclosed. That was it. I was almost shocked that there wasn't more of the typical voluminous amounts of packaging and waste that accompanies most products in today's marketplace.

Apple has clearly understood that this is of no benefit to the customer. I actually ended up feeling even better about the product when I saw how thoughtfully it was packaged with so little waste.

It's imperative that employees understand the eight wastes. It's imperative that they understand that the goal is to cut everything in half—not just make little incremental improvements. The incremental improvements are the tools we use to cut everything in half. Yet, they're always looking at the big picture as a result of the teaching and training we do on a daily basis in our morning meeting.

Global Lean is an important concept that I may have overlooked or not identified clearly enough in my previous writings, but I'm taking the time now to clarify. It is just as important to have a global perspective as it is to have a 2 second perspective. Both work in tandem to produce a successful culture and allow value to flow to the customer.

Another way we develop a global picture at FastCap is through the great diet of material that we digest on a regular basis in our teaching and training. Books like The Toyota Way, 14 Principles of Operational Excellence and Art Byrne's book, The Lean Turnaround are just a few examples of the DOZENS of books we read to improve our understanding of LEAN.

Recently, on my show The American Innovator, I said, "Our goal is for everything to be struggle-free—or to have zero struggle in every activity."

A listener, Shannon, wrote, "Wow! That makes Lean so tangible."

The idea that every activity should have "zero struggle" or be "struggle-free" means in Lean terminology that there should be no:

MURI = Burden or struggle
MURA = Unevenness or variation
MUDA = Waste which is the result of burden which produces unevenness or a lack of flow, which makes everything a struggle

If you have no burden, then you will have evenness, which reduces waste, removes the struggle and lets value flow to the customer. In layman's terms "zero struggle" sums up beautifully the goal of Lean and why it is so important that everything should flow.

Flow is exactly what 2 Second Lean delivers to the shop floor. 2 Second Lean is the "Lean" approach to implementing Lean. Lean is so much about flow and evenness. Kaizen events, while they have the ability to produce positive results—as they did in the early years at Fastcap—did not prove to be the best model for us. In my mind kaizen events are essentially the batch work application of Lean principles. They do not introduce flow to the shop floor; they are by nature disruptive. They require you to stop for a day, a week—or whatever it takes—for everyone to focus on a particular area. This creates unevenness and even a burden to the system.

I think the 2 Second Lean approach is successful because it just asks for small improvements on a daily basis at a prescribed time—the first thing in the morning before you begin your normal production. In doing that, you introduce flow to improvements and you don't introduce unevenness to the production floor. 2 Second Lean is the Lean principle applied in an even and consistent way that allows continuous improvement to flow through any organization.

Shannon also wrote, "What Lean all boils down to is this: Lean is really the golden rule—do unto others as you would want them to do unto you."

Lean makes the person doing the work a real-time advocate for the customer. The customer can't be on the shop floor making sure value is being delivered, but a well-trained Lean-thinking team member is the ultimate customer advocate. Lean is delivering to the customer only value-added activity. If you were the customer, that's what you would want. As a producer of anything, whether food, electronics, software, cars or medical care, my real role is a perpetual advocate on the shop floor for the customer. As a customer I can get very excited about the idea that any organization is focused that intently on serving me.

Global Lean has many facets, but real-time, shop-floor customer advocates might be the best example of Global Lean.

I have learned so much as a result of collaborating with others. I deliberately seek to give credit, not seek to get credit. The result is a dynamic collaborative culture, where everyone can learn and improve at every turn. Sam and Shannon, as well as thousands of others, have made a profound difference in helping me understand the power of being a Lean thinker.

Isaac, another listener and great Lean thinker, recently sent this email after watching an American Innovator show, "Paul, most adults have lost the child-like excitement you have about life and discovery. It is so refreshing to see how excited you are about life and the prospect of continuous learning."

I am excited about 2 Second Lean, Global Lean, Collaboration Lean, Advocate Lean, Golden Rule Lean—and dare I say Kindergarten Lean.

THE ONE THING:
LEAN IS THE GOLDEN RULE

Lean videos:

1. Interview with Hannah
http://youtu.be/JxmP5Nq15GI

2. Lean at Home 1
http://youtu.be/3F0R9iOH2_c

3. Lean at Home 2
http://youtu.be/zkIXuS2p6o0

Chapter 16

Lean is a Foreign Language

Often times when I speak I say things that can make people uncomfortable. I speak a business language that often seems like a foreign language. Here are a few of my favorite words—and what they mean to me.

Trust: the act of letting your people screw up.

I talk about trusting my people. It is very uncomfortable for most leaders to trust their people, because leaders rise to the position of leadership by having all the answers. They are leaders because of their business acumen, intelligence and their ability to get things done. They hire people to support those activities, but they seldom invite them to innovate as equals in the process. They rarely trust their people, and thus, they squelch an enormous amount of potential.

I trust my people and I know they'll fail just as I have. Most of my great advancements personally have come at the cost of me failing. Why would I not afford my own people the same opportunity and allow them to grow and experience these lessons in the same way that I have?

Trust is an important ingredient in developing a Lean culture and it's probably the one that makes people the most uncomfortable. They just don't want to take a chance on someone screwing it up. Screwing it up allows deep and serious learning, which translates into forward momentum that most companies and organizations desperately need. Leaders are looking for the edge, but it eludes them, because they refuse to trust their people.

Fanatical: embracing historical time-tested ideas with emotion and unstoppable resolve.

Most leaders think that you have to be even-tempered and can't get excited about anything. I am excited about everything, particularly life itself. For me, being fanatical is critical to being an effective leader. I am crazy about the adherence to the time-tested principles of relentlessly eliminating waste and growing people. I am a fanatic about Lean principles. Why? Because they work. They have always worked and they will continue to work for anyone who applies them with passion. They are the stuff that the greatest companies in the world are built on—and that is worth being a little fanatical over.

Toyota, Harley Davidson, Virginia Mason Hospital, Wire Mold, Southwest Airlines and a whole host of other companies have applied the principles of Lean thinking in a fanatical way—with a relentless pursuit of time-tested principles—and have produced astounding results. For these companies, Lean is not simply just another methodology or a tool in the tool box. It is a distinctive strategy that becomes all-consuming in everything they do.

Deflection: the act of honoring others

One of the most powerful concepts in becoming an effective Lean leader is the ability to deflect credit away from yourself and give it to others. It starts at the top, is modeled at the top and it must reside as the most strategic idea a leader has. When the top leader models it, others will do the same thing. It is in the act of deflecting that people engage the biggest skeptics. Taking credit for things repels people and suppresses a collaborative culture. Deflection is magical and top on the vocabulary list of effective Lean leadership.

Humanity: the act of recognizing the giftedness of others

Lean is supremely about people. We're in the business of changing and improving humanity. At its core, Lean is about nothing other than teaching, training, refining, learning, and improving the condition of people. Lean is not a mechanical system for eliminating waste. It's a methodology to change people's minds about the way they see work. Work is noble and we can do so much to elevate something we all do.

Audacious: the routine belief in the seemingly impossible

Lean thinkers are audacious. We are here to change the world. We are not here to create good, healthy businesses.

The goal of any Lean leader is much more than simply building a bottom line. We see the possibility that the Lean way of thinking can significantly improve the quality of people's lives. We are here to make that happen, and in the process, change the world.

Kata: the rhythm of work

We love routines that build excellence. Kata is a Japanese word that simply means routine. The routines that we deploy as Lean thinkers are the morning meeting and the 2 second daily improvement. The morning meeting creates clear communication among all team members. The 2 second daily improvement is the drum beat for a vibrant Lean culture.

Profit: the result of excellence

Perhaps one of the most controversial concepts I push is that we are not here to make money. Profit and money are a by-product of an effective Lean culture. We are here first and foremost to improve the quality of the customer's life. Internally, we are here to grow our people. If we do both of these at a high level, we will be profitable. However, profit is not the reason to do Lean nor is it the reason a company exists. If I told you the number of times I have encountered businesses that have gone south, with good products and capable people, you would be shocked. Ultimately the problem stems from the leadership focusing on profit and themselves, forgetting why the business exists in the first place. Take your mind off the numbers, focus on your customer, your people and serving others, and you will be surprised how everything else will work out.

Chapter 17

Organizing Waste

On a recent trip to Europe I had a Q & A session with a very thoughtful group of Lean bankers from Tatra Banka, the Slovak subsidiary of Vienna-based Raiffeisen Bank International. The questions were exceptional, so I thought I would dedicate a chapter to answering their inquiries and talking about their noteworthy brand of Lean. Bankers are the last place I would expect to find a vibrant Lean culture. Raiffeisen is big in Eastern Europe—seventeen countries and over 60,000 employees. The size alone would be formidable if one were trying to shift the culture to Lean thinking. Banking is not

Lean bankers

manufacturing, not that it matters, but it's certainly not the epicenter of Lean. Let's face it, bankers can be stiff and inflexible and not overly friendly—but not Raiffeisen.

In my twelve-year Lean journey, I have never met a group of people as on fire. They have a "come hell or high water, we're going to get this thing done" mentality. In addition, they are fun-loving, creative and very advanced in their understanding of how Lean works. For their Lean champions and Lean navigators, Lean is not a rigid business tool. Lean is a platform for creativity, innovation and lots of laughter. Here are three examples of Raiffeisen's Lean thinkers at work.

Upon arriving at their Lean forum, I learned about an evening event scheduled on one of the boats on the Danube. After drinks and dinner Leanne and I were informed of a team building exercise. Natalia, a board member of the bank, whispered, "You won't believe what they're about to do. They're going to have a Lean dress up, based on waste that we have collected. Each team is going to have to dress one individual in 'waste.' Let's see how creative they can be."

I thought, "Wow! That sounds interesting, but will it work?"

Well, after about an hour of each team working with great diligence, the catwalk was opened and the waste parade began. One after  another, contestants wearing the waste that is common to all of us—plastic bottles, newspaper, bubble wrap, cardboard, etc— had our full attention. It was about the funniest thing I've ever seen and illustrated so clearly how much waste exists and how easy it is to miss it. Hanging waste on a single individual really brings it to life. I

Waste dress-up

made a video because I thought the presentation was so powerful. It's called The Lean Catwalk. This is a great example of how a bank taught their people to think creatively about seeing waste and have fun at the same time.

A second example is Captain Bob and his three mates. The next day, they had Lean breakout sessions for all the Lean groups from seventeen different countries. One of them was unbelievable. There was Captain Bob, and the three mates that he had tied up with a rope. Each mate had a custom shirt denoting his kind of waste.

Captain Bob & 3 mates

There was First Mate Variability, with a hook on his arm. He was shouting in a pirate's voice, "I am stealing your profits and your customers!"

And then there was Second Mate Rigidity shouting, "I will steal your profitability. I am inflexible. Your customers' needs are not important. I will keep your customers from coming back."

The last mate had a shirt that read "Captain of the high seas." This was Captain Waste a Lot.

All three mates typified the attributes of non-Lean thinkers. Captain Bob had rounded them up and limited their influence on his ship. Poking fun at inconsistency and rigidity showed with great clarity the fastest way to kill your customers, business and profit. Clearly, Raiffeisen's Lean thinkers have a keen understanding of what Lean thinking can bring to the table, and they communicated it in a fun and memorable way.

Tie up the wastes

The third example is perhaps the funniest of all. One of the other

The lean guru

countries had a swami sitting down in a white robe with a sheet around his head. They called him "The Lean Guru." A girl was ringing a bell and saying, "Come ask the Lean Guru all your Lean questions." And of course a beautiful young girl was sitting on his lap.

People would come up and ask the swami, "How do I apply Lean in this situation?"

All I can say is that these people know how to have fun and I enjoyed both the visualization and the humor in making Lean relevant and fun. Raiffeisen understands that Lean is not just something you do. Lean is a strategy built around a strong culture of Lean thinking that can effectively let value flow to the customer.

When it came time for me to speak, one of the points I made was that Lean is not about being organized, because I was organized prior to becoming a Lean thinker. I had a beautiful facility that was buttoned down and was the quintessential example of what an organized facility should look like. I didn't understand the 8 wastes and my factory was a great example of overproduction—and still is in varying degrees. I had effectively "organized waste." When I asked the group if there was anything I said that was maybe a little shocking or interesting, Petra raised her hand and said, "Yes, this whole thing about being organized—and that it is not really Lean."

Petra

I replied, "You can organize waste." And then I looked at the slide I had

Organized waste

just shown of my shelves filled with inventory—perfectly polished, shined and predictable, well-labeled and good visual controls—all the elements of Lean. But unfortunately, the inventory was waste. It was an example of overproduction, and overproduction is where all waste begins. I efficiently organized waste!

So, if you overproduce as I was doing prior to understanding Lean, and frankly still do, then it doesn't matter how well-organized it is, you still have organized waste. I think for Petra, that was a revelation, because many Lean thinkers spend a lot of time making sure everything is perfectly organized. I know I'm guilty of that, but we must realize that organizing something is not indicative of being Lean. Lean is eliminating waste or non-value-added activity. Anything that doesn't add value to the customer is waste. The customer wants the product. They don't want to have to pay for me to make it, transport it, put it on a shelf, manage it, power and heat the building to store it, light the shelves and then pay for all my employees to go up and down and count inventory once a month. That is total waste. Organized... but, total waste.

The title of my talk was "Lean is Simple." At the end of the talk one of the participants asked me a fantastic question, "What is the most important Lean improvement you've ever made?"

I thought, "Wow! Nobody has ever asked me that." I had to pause and think, because we have made so many great Lean improvements. The top improvement was when we switched from doing kaizen events to making 2 second improvements. It was at that moment that I got everybody to buy in.

We did that by simply asking people to fix what bugs them, to look at each of their work areas and ask, "Is everything perfect? You wouldn't change a single thing? Surely there must be something that irritates the hell out you?" Getting people to think at this level about what bugs them and then make the effort to improve it or fix it—no matter how small the improvement—was the single most important improvement I made.

Prior to 2 Second Lean, Lean required me to organize kaizen events. Someone had to organize an event, manage a kaizen newspaper and a variety of other kaizen tools. But when I simply said, "Stop the struggle. Fix what bugs you and make a 2 second improvement," that was the game changer for FastCap.

As the hands continued to rise, another girl heard me say, "Everywhere I go I see waste. It doesn't matter whether I'm buying a hot dog on the streets of Prague or in a conference center like this, I see waste. And that has been very important to my success. I see waste everywhere. I've trained my eyes to see it." This young woman raised her hand and asked one of the best questions. Instead of pointing at me, she asked, "Where do you see the waste in us?"

Where is my waste?

This is an example of a mature Lean culture. They are comfortable enough to be able to ask me where I see their waste. When I speak I usually take five or six Mini iPoles and Super Mounts, one of the products that I developed to do Lean filmmaking, and I give them to people who ask me great questions. Needless to say, I promptly gave her one. And I asked the audience, "Why did I choose to give the Mini iPoles and Super Mount for this question, over all the other questions that I've been asked this evening?"

She replied in typical Raiffeisen humor, "Because I am beautiful." A hearty laughter arose.

There were quite a few other answers, but finally somebody got it. "It's because she focused on herself and her own problems."

Exactly! This is one of the most difficult things for any culture to do. The sign of a mature culture is being comfortable asking the questions, "What is it that I need to improve? Where is my waste? What do you see?"

Lean filming

I think this is a revealing question. As I reflect on the success that FastCap has had in implementing 2 Second Lean and building a Lean culture, I think one of the most important things has been our relentless willingness to ask our customers where we are failing and how we can improve. We ask that both of our customers and internally of one another. We're not threatened by someone saying, "You know, I think there might be a better way to do that." or "Bob, are you sure that's a Lean methodology that you are applying there?" And nine times out of ten there's no defensiveness, just an eagerness to improve. This is a clear milestone in building any Lean culture. And in the Q & A session, this girl did such a beautiful job of reflecting how we should all approach improvement.

Now remember, as I'm telling these stories, I'm talking about a bank. This is not the place you would expect to find such forward thinking in Lean. Next I was asked, "How do you teach a six-year-old Lean?" I thought this was another great question.

It just so happened that the next slide cued up was about the kids from Cornerstone Christian School and how they implemented Lean and made before-and-after videos. I showed the video and said, "It's very simple. You get kids to see a problem, and then you allow them to create

Cornerstone Christian School kids

a solution and encourage them to make before-and-after videos. When you do that the Lean experience becomes fun and relevant. This is how to teach a six-year-old—make it relevant and make it fun!

One of my favorite improvements is from a six-year-old, Katie Bailey. Katie was having a problem getting to the school bus on time in the morning. Her father, a Lean thinker, suggested that she stop and ask the question, "What is causing the problem that makes you late?"

Katie

"Well, Papa, in the morning I can't find my backpack."

"Why can't you find your backpack?"

"Because I always leave it around somewhere and I don't know where I leave it."

"Why don't we find a special place to put your backpack so it's always in the same place?"

So, before long Katie's wheels were spinning, and she established a specific place where her backpack goes every night before she goes to bed. Now, in the morning when she wakes up, she gets ready, brushes her teeth, goes to the post, picks up her backpack and is no longer late for school.

This is how you teach a six-year-old Lean thinking. Let them solve the problem and give them ownership of the solution. Ask questions, allow them to solve their problems and make it fun and relevant.

Can you imagine the kind of leader, employee, or business owner that Katie Bailey will be when she grows up? At an early age she is learning to solve problems and eliminate waste through continuously improving everything.

The next comment, though, is one of my favorites. I'll close this chapter with this one. I ask people in the audience, "How does Lean make you feel or how do you feel about Lean?" Not everybody is a hundred percent behind the Lean way of thinking.

Lucia, a young woman in the back, raised her hand. "Lean makes you smile even at work."

My response was, "Why do you feel that way?"

"Because Lean makes my life easier. Lean makes my life happier. Lean makes me more confident. Lean makes me the owner of my future." Who could express Lean better than that?

Lucia

Lean has been misunderstood to be the methodology of taking away jobs, making things sterile with little or no creativity. Lean is the opposite of that. Rarely, if ever, does it take away a single job. It creates boundless opportunities and continual employment, adds longevity for existing employees and growth for new people to be brought into the company. That's the way it works at FastCap.

My response was, "When you are a Lean thinker, you are a sought-after commodity." I would venture to say, "Wherever Lucia goes, if she remains a strong Lean thinker, every organization will recognize her—and other Lean thinkers—as an invaluable asset."

This Q & A session at Tatra Banka was one of the best I've ever had from one of the most engaged groups of people I've ever encountered. They made it fun, they made Lean relevant, and they weren't afraid to ask tough questions and be reflective about their own actions. Above all else, the leadership at Raiffeisen is remarkable, you know who you are….Great job! My hat is off to you!

THE ONE THING:
LEAN MAKES YOU THE OWNER OF YOUR FUTURE.

Lean videos:

1. Katie's Bookbag
http://youtu.be/lp66VBZsZqI

2. The American Innovator: Kindergarten Lean
http://youtu.be/e8G0QOWUS_Q

3. Waste Runway
http://youtu.be/VBE94oKH5Vc

Chapter 18

The Real Juice of Lean

We have a principle at our company that simply states, "There are two kinds of people in the world—givers and takers." Our goal should be to eliminate all the takers out of our lives as fast and as furiously as we can and be a profound giver to all humanity.

Another way of saying it is, "There are two kinds of people in the world, happy people who are focused on the happiness of others and people who are unhappy because they are focused on their own happiness—givers and takers."

It is a profound concept that I've really come to grips with in the course of my life that has differentiated how I conduct myself in every situation. I am not negotiating the advantage. I think in terms of creating a win-win with an emphasis on helping others. I've found that every time I act as a servant, life gets better, and when I look for what's in it for me, life gets ugly. In applying this principle to Lean, I've found the same to be true. The real juice from Lean comes when you start giving back.

We've created a Lean organization whose primary focus is to
1. Serve and deliver value to our customers
2. Grow and fully develop our people internally
3. Give back to the community and strengthen the business environment.

These three activities will help and improve the quality of people's lives around the world and that is exciting.

At FastCap, our Lean activity has not been done for profit. In large measure, we give away the preponderance of the books that we print.

We give away the audio file regularly. We give away the digital file regularly. We provide tours of our facility at no charge, but at great expense to our company's time and resources. In doing so, our people are elevated and we are elevating the lives of others. Our people feel as though they're making a contribution. They feel positive about themselves and about their ability to make a difference. We are creating an environment where people are operating at a higher level than traditionally would be expected in an organization. We have made our company all about giving—and giving back.

When an organization sets out to incorporate or build a Lean culture, it is a great undertaking. And that undertaking will be amplified when the company begins to teach, train, and facilitate Lean practices outside of their organization. That is when we first experienced the real juice of Lean. Approximately six or seven years ago, we began to let people tour our crummy little facility that had flaws from top to bottom. Every

Give a tour and give back

time someone toured our facility, we learned more about our own waste and our own deficiencies and became aware of more opportunities to improve what we were doing. In doing so, we not only helped the people coming to tour the facility, but we received the benefit of new eyes looking at our activities. To this day, we continue to do that and we do it with intensity and purpose, because we know that the real juice comes from Lean when you start giving back.

THE ONE THING:
GIVING IS GREATER THAN RECEIVING

Chapter 19

90% is Waste

What a staggering statement. Most people say, "No way, Paul, I am very productive!"

Then I retort, "You and I are extremely productive at producing non-value-added activity."

Since the dawn of time man has been in pursuit of being more productive. Just think of all the great innovations like the wheel, windmill, steam engine, automobile, and airplane. It is in our DNA to improve, but the way we improve and the processes we deploy, can also be very efficient waste generators.

In the Lean world there is something we call the spaghetti trail. A simple Lean exercise would be to chart the walking path of how a particular person would travel to perform a common task, like emptying the dishwasher. Most of us are shocked at the amount of non-valve activity (walking, reaching, opening and closing) compared to the value-added activity (getting the dishes and silverware in the cabinets and drawers). The actual value-added time is a millisecond compared to all the waste.

Spaghetti trail

The same is true of the computer jock who spends most of their time clicking on the computer and searching for documents, as opposed to adding value and changing and improving something. I am acutely aware of waste and many times I see ten emails exchanged by me and my associates when it should have taken one or two at the most. Ninety percent of everything you and I do every day is waste. That is just a statistical reality.

Human beings have a natural capacity to create and develop and improve. However, it is essential that we develop and utilize this to

Computer jocks

its full potential. We are problem solvers at our core, at the very design of the way we were made. But more often than not, we don't tap into this innate potential, because we don't have a good process to harness it. We are not ants that go in and just grab a grain of sand, pull it out, stack it, and dig a hole. We go in, grab the grain of sand, pull it out, stack it and have the capacity to ask, "How can I do it better?" and we build an excavator. The key is to create a strategy, a deliberateness, a methodology that taps into that God-given genius. Perhaps that is why I'm so passionate about Lean, because it does exactly that. It is a system that taps into the genius that God infused and designed into all of us.

Perhaps the most powerful story I can use to illustrate the amount of waste in processes and the effectiveness of a Lean strategy, is the story of our graphic design department. I must admit that I have never found it easy to work with graphic designers. They are more prone to the artistic side and often lack a natural predilection to process improvements.

At one point we had two full-time graphic designers and were always backlogged with work. As I would work with them I noticed an excessive amount of opening and closing files, and searching for files and copy. I couldn't understand how this process could be so convoluted. When I would question them about it they would respond by saying that it is just how graphic design works. I knew it could be improved dramatically. Regardless of how much I taught them about Lean and prodded them to improve the process, I was not successful in getting the significant process improvements.

Finally, my frustration was too much for one of the designers and she quit. Yes, this is an example of Paul being a bad leader...I never said I was perfect! The second one had to be dismissed. Instead of hiring another professional, I brought in Graham from the shop floor. He was a self-trained graphic designer who had been working on the shop floor and making 2 second improvements—and doing an exceptional job at it. Remember, he was not a formally trained graphic designer. In a matter of weeks he was able to learn the necessary skills, figure out where things were stored and catch up where we were behind. Finally, I had someone who applied Lean to the graphic design department and now, not only were we caught up, but he had turned a two-person full-time job into a one-person job with time to spare. Today, most jobs get done within an hour of the time they are given to him. He is relentless about improvement. I can't remember the last time I had to ask him to make an improvement, because he employs the Lean principles with every mouse click. Not only does he accomplish the design job of two people, but he helps out in three other significant departments on a daily basis.

This illustrates how 90 percent of what we do is waste. There are endless opportunities to eliminate the waste and let value flow to our internal and external customers.

Chapter 20

Lean All-Stars

I'm told over and over again by mid-level managers …"My boss doesn't get it and won't support what I'm trying to do." My reply is always the same; "focus on yourself, develop your own area of influence and be relentless about continuous improvement in your life. If you adopt this approach, in short order you will not only rise up and be promoted, but you will eventually be the leader of your organization or another thoughtful organization that understands the power of true Lean leadership."

Lean leadership is not a little different than other leadership, it is fundamentally different. Typical leaders are concerned about themselves and their position and status. The Lean leader is always thinking of the people they are responsible for and how they can teach, train, improve and better the lives of everyone. This is servant leadership at the highest level. It is rare and is a sought-after trait.

On an almost regular basis I am asked if I know of any Lean leaders who would like a job managing and running a major organization. Unfortunately, the answer is almost always no. You see, I have met and come across hundreds of green belt and black belt Lean certified practitioners, however, few have the capacity to inspire people to greatness. Just today I was asked again if I knew of someone who I would recommend to step into a position of Lean leadership in a major corporation. I replied back that I could only think of one person with the qualifications for the job. His name is Bruce. Below is Bruce's reply to me and it is the essence of this chapter. When you "get" Lean leadership you are the bomb, a rare breed, and the sky is the limit.

Hi Paul.

Thank you for thinking of me for this position. I am honored! It sounds like a terrific company.

Like you, I am also reluctant to recommend anyone UNLESS that person is a genuine Lean all-star. I know several Lean practitioners, but frankly very, very few possess the dynamic, engaging personality you need to inspire and excite a workforce to embrace a cultural migration to Lean. I feel it is unethical to recommend a Lean practitioner just because they are a friend or an associate.

I know just one person who I think would excel at this position, but as you might expect, he is well paid (approx. $200K/YR) and really loves his job and his life in Mississippi.

Sorry I was unable to provide any solid leads.

-Bruce

I recommended Bruce for the job not because he showed me graphs and charts of statical data about all their Lean success. He didn't try to wow me with Lean terms or Japanese concepts. He didn't recite to me all the companies he transformed under his great Leadership. I met Bruce at a talk that I gave. He came to learn, even though he had 15 years more experience then I did. He sat at a table in the front row with 5 or 6 of his people and they were all smiles; giddy about Lean! They were happy because their culture, not their Lean tools and terms, was central to their success. This is how I measure Lean success. I have never seen a culture like this that didn't produce astounding stats, but I have seen a lot of stats and no culture. Be a Lean all-star; you will be loved appreciated and compensated beyond your wildest imagination.

When I go to hire someone, I always hire for character and teach for skill. I can teach anybody to do the job, but character is a rare commodity. I have recently developed a new way to screen people who are interested in working for Fastcap. I ask them to send me a quick 2 to 3 minute video telling me about themselves. You can learn so much from how people respond to this request. All-stars have no problem, say they have never done it before but they'll figure it out and send it right over. Others hesitate and come up with reasons why they don't want to do it. This simple assignment reveals so much about people. At the same time, it allows you to meet a lot more people so you can more efficiently make thoughtful decisions about potential new team members.

Below is a sample of the video resume I did demonstrating how easy it is to make this happen on your iPhone. The second video resume is from Graham, one of our all-stars who's moving to the Denver area. While I regret the fact that we are losing Graham, I'm going out of my way to help him find a phenomenal company where he can continue to have a huge impact because of his deep understanding of how to build lean culture.

Once again, the use of video is a powerful tool that sets you apart from everyone else. They say if you want to get someone's attention, you have to be remarkable. Doing things the old way is not remarkable. Sending a video resume is, at the very least, extremely interesting and, to most people, remarkable.

Learning to communicate in this edgy and interesting way makes you an all-star and that's not a bad position to be in!

THE ONE THING:
ALL-STARS LOVE PEOPLE AND INSPIRE THEM

Paul's Example of a Video Resume
http://youtu.be/bF7rOuBQDok

Graham's All-Star Video Resume
http://youtu.be/nZ-n1KAbN_l

Chapter 21

Make Lean Blast Off

Most people reject "simple" because it smacks them in the face when they refuse to take action. If you add complexity to anything it slows action down, muddles the path forward, and will flummox the brightest minds. These are my top 11 steps to supercharge any Lean culture, in the order of importance. If your culture lacks energy and power, go back to step 1 and repeat until you experience nuclear fusion.

1 - The CEO or president must embrace Lean personally and not delegate it to the team to implement.

2 - Meet regularly as a team, preferably once a day, to address issues, talk about improvements and problems, and teach Lean principles. You wouldn't play the Super Bowl without meeting as a team and strategizing. At FastCap, we treat every day as if we are playing the Super Bowl. This way, we win the hearts and minds of our customers and improve the performance of the team.

3 - Learn and teach the 8 wastes. Everyone in the company should know them by heart without memorizing an acronym. They should understand it. Waste always starts with overproduction, then transportation, then inventory, then there's a defect, then you have to repair the defect, creating the waste of over-processing and motion, while the customer is waiting and you're wasting your God-given ability to make improvements and change the world.

4- Make simple before and after videos of all your improvements. Start a YouTube channel and the concept will spread like wildfire through your organization. Keep it simple. The video should be made with your smartphone. Don't buy camera equipment or expensive software. It is important that you do it immediately when you see the potential for an improvement. Don't batch work- don't delay. Perfection is a curse!

5 - Don't ever point to somebody else and say, "look at all their waste." Always point at yourself. You have enough waste in your own life for 10 lifetimes! I can't tell you the number of times executives come up to me after I speak and bemoan the waste of others in their organizations. I just look them in the eye and say, "the problem is you. This starts and ends with you. Stop telling me about how you need to change everyone else. The problem is you. Lead and people will follow; point and people will run."

6 - Can't find something to improve? Simply fix what bugs you. Fix everything you struggle with. Anything that is not flowing is an easy opportunity to improve. I can find 10 clunky processes in the first hour I spend with anyone, including myself.

7 - Where should you start? How should you find these potential improvements? Look for anywhere work is stopped. Work should never stop, it should always flow. If it stops, there is waste.

8 - Do I need someone to help me? Should I hire a consultant? The answer is hell no! If you do hire a consultant, it will guarantee your dependence on somebody else. Becoming a Lean thinker is easy despite what anybody tells you. If you learn this on your own, it will be deeply embedded in the way you think about everything. All consultants are not bad. In fact many are good. Most consultants are misused. Never hire a consultant to bring Lean to your organization. Hire a consultant to tweak and improve a vibrant culture. If a consultant takes you to the conference room, show them the door and run like hell! The work is where the work is done: in the office or on the shop floor, not in a conference room.

9 - Never try to get your family to do Lean. Do it yourself and do it well and you will become a magnet to every thoughtful person on the planet. This is why step 1 is so important. See the video at the end of this chapter.

10 - What if I'm not the top leader in my organization? How can I affect change and build a Lean culture? Regardless of your station in life, every human being has influence over something and someone. Build Lean in that sphere of influence and you will be elevated to the top leader in short order.

11 - Never look for the complex solution to solve a problem. Always pursue the simple and elegant one. Use your head, not your wallet!

> # THE ONE THING:
> ## LEAN IS FUN. IF THERE'S NO FUN,
> ## YOU'RE MISSING THE DESSERT OF LIFE

Weekend Lean
http://youtu.be/gHlnhjea61w

Chapter 22

Video Afterburner

This chapter is all about marketing Lean. We have literally had thousands of companies around the world implement the 2 second model by making Lean simple and fun. The question now is how to put your fun culture on afterburners? The reason why so many cultures have had such great luck with implementing Lean is because they have been deliberate about the implementation. They developed a consistent pattern of daily:

- 3S-ing
- 2 second improvements
- A morning meeting
- Before and after videos

I have now been to over 50 countries. My travel allows me to see all different kinds of organizations. This exposure allows me to see small ways to make improvements that can make a profound difference in my company and others. I noticed one organization who has made over 2000 improvement videos but the viewership on these videos was not as high as I think it should've been. They were great videos, the employees produced them with great energy and creativity, but the entire team had not seen them and my natural thought was, what a waste! Everyone should see these videos, they are fantastic. They need to ask some questions; Is there an organized way that you guys can disseminate this information? Is there a deliberate practice by which people are getting all these amazing videos to get ideas from?

At Fastcap we've applied Lean to the way we do everything, especially our marketing. Once a week we send out a 2 second Lean email blast to people around the world to see all the cool improvements that people are making.

Lean E-Blast

Once a week we send out a product email blast so our customers can see all the new innovations that we are continually coming out with. The results have been nothing short of amazing. The best part is it's easy to do because we created templates for these email blasts and then all we have to do is send them out to the assigned distribution list.

I wondered why each respective company doesn't send out their own 2 second Lean improvement videos to their internal staff in a deliberate way? I have begun suggesting to organizations to send out a weekly email blast with the great videos that are being produced by their team to the rest of the team's e-mails. As you would expect, the results have been fantastic.

The key is to make these email blasts:

- Simple
- Very few words
- Visible video link to click on
- Personal: always have them addressed to the person who's receiving the email i.e. Hi Paul
- If possible always ask a question. "Can you believe Bob saved this much time? Check out the video below and see how he did it."

This is deliberate practice on steroids. On the next page, you'll find an example of our Lean e-blast. Feel free to copy anything you want. The results will be Lean on an afterburner!

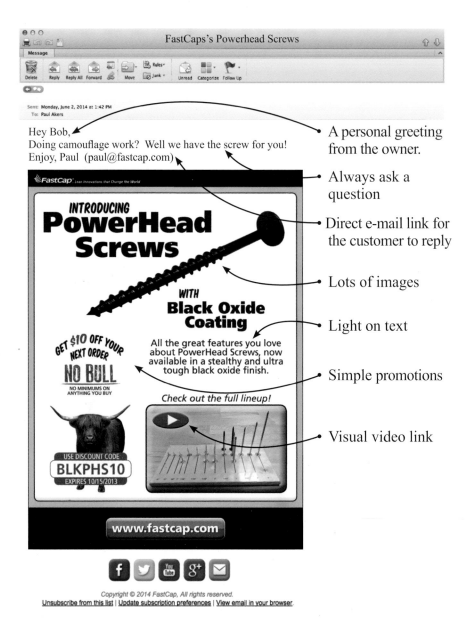

A personal greeting from the owner.

Always ask a question

Direct e-mail link for the customer to reply

Lots of images

Light on text

Simple promotions

Visual video link

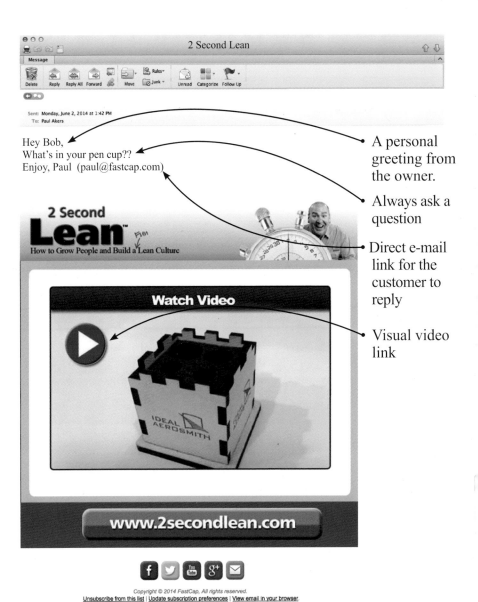

Hey Bob,
What's in your pen cup??
Enjoy, Paul (paul@fastcap.com)

A personal greeting from the owner.

Always ask a question

Direct e-mail link for the customer to reply

Visual video link

Chapter 23

Our New

Building for the future

After years of waiting and planning, we've finally finished our 50,000 square foot temple to Lean, our new factory in Ferndale, Washington. Every detail was designed with the employees and customers in mind.

Paul had dreamed about constructing a state of the art building for years,

but with the economic downturn of 2008, the building project was put on the hold. Thanks to Extreme Lean, we continued to grow. The building project resumed early in 2013 and we moved in at the end of the year.

Our new building is packed full of Lean innovations. One of the most important Lean principles, *respect for people*, is evident everywhere you look. The facility features 110 windows for natural light, automatic LED lighting, radiant heat, Big Ass Fans™, and an integrated Bose™ sound system. Every day feels like summer!

Chef's Kitchen

We also built a top-of-the-line chef's kitchen for employee use. With the best quality appliances and cabinets, our people feel respected and appreciated. You can often smell something baking when you walk by.

Our woodworker roots are obvious the minute you walk through the door. Beautiful exposed beams and pine trim extend throughout the building. The 1200 square-foot woodshop is our playground and you'll always find someone in there.

Wood Shop - Our Playground

The bathrooms at FastCap have always been our pride and joy so when it came time to design them for the new facility, we pulled out all the stops. In our old building, people

The Bathroom - Our Pride & Joy

had to waste motion walking to five different bathrooms. Those bathrooms were often occupied without any way of knowing before checking the door handle. To eliminate the waste, we built the new bathroom in a single location with multiple private stalls. This eliminated excess motion by having to walk to different locations.

We also added a light system to alert people when a stall is occupied. Because the lights are visible from anywhere in the building, people can easily see when bathroom stalls

Bathroom Lights

become available. These two Lean improvements have saved us hours of wasted motion every day.

In addition to making the new building

Completely Private Bathroom Stalls

the best possible place to work, we designed it so that all work would flow smoothly through it. There are no walls in the facility apart from the bathroom, woodshop, and a small conference and server room. This allows us absolute flexibility when designing workflow and also allows us to adapt to any future needs.

No Walls

The facility was also designed to be easy to clean and maintain.

Engineering & Production Cells on Wheels

Instead of carpet, tile, and concrete floors, we used polished concrete throughout. This allows us to standardize cleaning processes and supplies. Now cleaning is fun, fast, and easy.

Every workstation and production cell in the building is on wheels. This allows us to adapt to any situation that our work calls for. If we need to move production closer to shipping, we can do it in minutes rather than days. Everything from engineering to production to the main office is mobile and modular.

Our people are on wheels too! Because our new building is so much larger than our previous facility, we needed to come up with a way to get around efficiently. Our fleet of basket-equipped Razor®

A Full Scooter Station

scooters allow us to get from one end of the building to the other in under 30 seconds.

All of our offices feature stand up desks. Because there aren't any walls, it's easy to stay on the same page. The desks are arranged in quadrants

Stand Up Office

that encourage collaboration and you'll often see people ganging up to tackle projects and answer questions. There are no opportunities for waste to build up in this office!

Graphic Design Department

The graphic design department is open to the floor, making it easy to change packaging and marketing materials on the fly as needs arise.

Standardized Carts & Stations

Most of our workstations are built out of our FastPipe, a system of steel pipes and connectors. Because we use standard building materials, we can adapt any station according to our needs. It also allows us to build modular carts, tables, and stations that are easy to duplicate and modify. If a station is no longer needed, we can recycle the materials and turn them into something else. We can put the needs of our customers first and deliver better products faster, at a reduced cost because we're not married to expensive or fixed workstations.

Our Order Station

The inventory racking is laid out with $5^{1}/_{2}$ foot wide aisles, allowing us to store our inventory in half the space of conventional racking. Built-in guidance systems allow the forklift to safely operate at full speed. At the end of each inventory rack are the production cells for all the products in the aisle. This allows flow from the inventory of raw products to finished goods before the inventory even leaves the aisle.

All the Lean improvements implemented during design and construction have lead to huge increases in productivity across the board.

Narrow Aisles

We're putting out the highest quality products we've ever produced and our volume has increased, all while our work has become even easier and more enjoyable. It's all thanks to Lean!

Want to see more? Check out our video tour below! Here's a response from one of our raving fans:

> *Just wanted to say I've watched a couple videos on your new facility and it is amazing. You and your team are doing phenomenal work! I know you're never done, but your work continues to inspire. Please make sure your team knows that the efforts you put into the process every day are inspiring people here in Pennsylvania. I know the recipe for success requires excellent leadership and an excellent team. You guys ROCK and make me proud of American Manufacturing and what is capable of being done in this country. Keep up the excellent work. You are a role model for me!*

Shawn Gross
Engineering & Materials Manager
Viking Plastics

THE ONE THING:
BUILD IT IN AND IT IS DIFFICULT TO CHANGE

Take a Lean Tour with Paul!
http://youtu.be/jYby_HczyDA

Chapter 24

Let's Take a Tour

Everyday I get approximately three speaking and/or tour requests. We now do 24 tours a year and the requirements are deliberately stiff in order to weed out anyone who is not serious about building a Lean culture. ***We are not teaching how to do Lean, we are teaching how to build a Lean culture***. With so much demand to learn, we had to come up with a Lean way to reach as many people as possible. I took my video camera and Razor scooter and spent 4 hours of my time producing a video tour. No professional video production crew, just me, my people, a Sony PJ 790 video camera, and my Mac with Final Cut Pro. It was simple, fast and easy but it is not perfect! Perfection is for people who want to tell you all the reasons they can't get things done. This video is designed to give you an overview of the way we think. We have almost 1000 videos (with over 1 million combined views) that are free online and go into all the details of any Lean subject.

There are so many companies around the world that are doing a Fantastic job of building a Lean Culture. This year I interviewed the the leaders of those companies at the MAPP conference in Indiana. You can find the Lean Roundtable Interview at the end of this chapter.

6 Lean Culture Building Companies

Walters &Wolfe	California
Xylem Design	Colorado
Klime-Ezee	UK
YelloTools	Germany
Viking Plastic	Pennsylvania
Omni Duct	California

Tour requirements

- CEO must be present. We understand that some organizations are huge and it is not likely that the CEO would attend the tour, however, you should know that we have had companies with 70,000 employees globally and the president, as well as the board members, have attended the tours many times. We have made exceptions to this stipulation, but only if we are convinced that the leader attending has the power to build a Lean culture successfully.
- Attendees must read this book, 2 Second Lean.
- Attendees must watch at least 10 of our Lean videos in advance.
- Be committed to transforming your culture and company to a Lean model in 1 year.
- Make 50 improvement videos (before/after) in the first year.
- Set up a public YouTube channel to share what you learn (Lean videos) with the world.
- Have other businesses tour your facility within 1 year of your FastCap tour (pay it forward)!
- The first thing you will do on the tour is cLean our bathrooms. This teaches humility, and demonstrates effective processes... two of the cornerstones of Lean.

If you can meet the above criteria these are the details for the tour:

- Reply to me with the names of attendees.
- We work in a manufacturing facility so warm clothes on cold days are encouraged; our plant is usually around 62 degrees.
- I recommend that you watch the following 8 videos so you will all have a good point of reference to maximize your visit. You can also visit our 2 Second Lean website where you will find many more videos and resources that you can use as training tools for your team.

Why FastCap Gives Lean Tours

- We have benefited so much from learning the Toyota Production System. This is our way of giving back.
- We want others to receive the same benefits we have in building a strong business climate in America.
- Toyota openly taught us their 50 years of experience for free, so we are paying it forward and doing the same thing.
- Our people get better at Lean when we teach it.
- Our people feel very rewarded and satisfied when others want to see and experience what we are doing to build a Lean culture.

FastCap's Expectations for People Touring

- Attendees should come with one clear goal of what they want to achieve.
- As you learn and implement Lean, our expectation is that you pay it forward by teaching others within one year of your visit to FastCap..
- The tour is not for the curious - it is for people who seriously want to learn Lean and have made a commitment to take what they learn and implement it.
- The tour must have senior leaders in attendance (owners, presidents, COO, etc.) Others are welcome to join.
- All attendees must have a commitment to Lean.

Getting Started After the Tour

- First of all, Lean is easy. Approach it with this mind set and you will succeed.
- Stop making excuses why you can't do it. If you make excuses, you will never learn or experience Lean. Change yourself, change your family, change your street, change your city, and change the world.
- Experience a Lean culture by touring Lean companies.
- Become part of the Lean family of businesses. Get connected.

We are all here to help one another.
- Experience it first, see the benefits with your own eyes, then begin to read and learn about it.
- Watch all the Lean videos FastCap provides and use them as training tools in your company.
- Read *The Toyota Way*.
- Sign up and listen to weekly broadcasts, *The American Innovator* and *2 Second Lean*. All past shows are available on iTunes as podcasts and on the website.

Remember, Lean is an endless journey.
My hope is that you enjoy your Lean
journey as much as I have enjoyed
mine. Life's an Adventure!

THE ONE THING:
DON'T LEARN LEAN. LEARN HOW TO BUILD A LEAN CULTURE.

FastCap's Lean Video Library

More Videos on the Next Page

MAPP Roundtable Interview
http://youtu.be/E9Na_YMKdvE

Walters & Wolf: Where's Shop B?
http://youtu.be/cqojZ-3aCKI

Xylem Design: Factory Tour
http://youtu.be/6IUywb_O2KU

Klime-Ezee: Lean Journey
http://youtu.be/NDZ1Cmhy3eE

Omniduct: Lean Blog

Viking Plastics: Lean Journey
http://youtu.be/dNCfKVQifbU

Weekly Broadcast Sign-up

Lean in a Nutshell
http://bit.ly/pCOvvq

Lean in a Nutshell!

1. Continuous improvement comes from "fixing what bugs you" every day!
2. Lean is all about the elimination of the 8 deadly wastes.
   - Overproduction
   - Overprocessing
   - Motion
   - Waiting
   - Transportation
   - Inventory
   - Rework of Defects
   - Unused Employee Genius
3. Waste is eliminated through continuous improvement.

Important Lean Principles

1. Lean thinkers encourage other people's creativity and respect for people.
2. Lean thinkers don't own ideas; it is always a team effort.
3. Lean thinkers say they are wrong at least 2 times a day.
4. Improvements are endless because waste is like gravity.
5. 90% of everything you do is waste.
6. Never look at the waste of others; you will always have plenty of your own!
7. Lean is not about working fast, but rather working smooth.

7 Magic Bullets to Building a Lean Culture

1. Teaching and training people.
2. The 2 second improvement every day from everyone.
3. Daily Morning 3S: Sweep, Sort and Standardize.
4. Start a daily morning meeting.
5. Start your Lean journey in the bathroom.
6. Start your Lean journey slowly.
7. Never start your lean journey until you are 1000% sure it is the right direction for you. If you do start prior to this understanding, you will fail.

The Results of Building a Lean Culture

1. Operational excellence
2. Low turnover
3. Customer retention
4. Consistent reduction in cost
5. Consistent increase in quality
6. Continuous innovation
7. A fun place to work

Lean Morning Meeting Agenda
Sample Pages

Morning Meeting Agenda

- 7:30-7:55 Leader preps for the meeting
- 7:55 Leader Announces over intercom and walkie-talkie 5 minutes until morning meeting
- 8:00 Good morning FastCap!
- 8:01 Announce tomorrow's Meeting Leader
- 8:02 Sales Numbers
- 8:03 Mistakes and discussion
- 8:10 Raving Fans
- 8:15 Product Review
- 8:20 Improvement
- 8:25 FastCap Principles
- 8:30 History and Enrichment
- 8:35 Constitution
- 8:40 Stretching
- 8:45 Back to Work

Note:

1. The times are approximate. Our morning meeting generally takes 30 minutes, but can take up to an hour depending on subjects and issues of the day.
2. We have the morning meeting every morning. We do not miss it. It is the most important way we build our culture. In the beginning, our morning meetings were only 5 minutes long. We recommend that you start the same way and make it sustainable.
3. Constant review and testing of the material you cover is critical for retention.
4. We are often asked if we have new employee orientation. The answer is "No." The morning meeting provides daily orientation and is infinitely more effective.

Leader: Our goal is for people to rave about our company. This is where emails and letter are read out loud to recognize our team for exceptional service.

Raving Fans

Examples of how FastCap blows people away!!

Example Letters

1. "Hi Kenzie! I want you to know that I am very grateful for what you did for me. You provided such friendly customer service and went the extra mile. Please forward this message to your supervisor. I want to extend a compliment to an excellent employee!"
Thanks, Lisa

2. "Hi Paul! Thank you for opening up your doors and letting us in for the Learn to See Lean Tour. Being able to see what you do is encouraging and impressive. I have seen my fair share of "World Class" companies over the years and your company by far has been one of the best.. hands down.
   We are considering ourselves lucky to be able to tour with you and Jon in Japan. Please convey our group's big "Thank you" to your employees. Their passion for continuous improvement and working together slapped me in the face the minute we walked in the door. Kudos!"
Jack Louie

3. "Hi FastCap! I just wanted to thank you for all your support. I am proud to be selling your line, the name is like selling Kleenex.. the name is so recognized. Your staff does an excellent job and is very helpful and customer driven."
Thanks, Roger York

4. "Hi Jenny! Geez, you make it hard to stay mad. You (and FastCap) have provided absolutely outstanding customer service. I received the HOD's today – TODAY, the day after our last communication. Before I opened my little handyman business, I spent decades providing and managing customer support operations in the computer industry. I would have LOVED to have had an employee like you.
Thanks for restoring my faith in (at least one) American business."
Don Meyers

5. "Hi Clint! Thank you for escorting me through your facility today for our annual safety audit. As usual, your facility stands front and center in tidiness. Your record keeping is impeccable and always up-to-date, and all the personnel are always aware of each others' presence and safety awareness. My rating gives you an A-. It is rare for me to hand out A's."
Frank Enriquez

Leader: Every day review one of our products so that our team is well-trained with hands-on information.

Product Review

The leader should be prepared to do the following:

1. Refer to the catalog to find the next product to be reviewed.
2. Go to our website and queue up the product video (when available).
3. Get the product to explain and pass around a sample.
4. Talk to Paul/Mike/Andrey/Jon about any additional technical info and additional demonstration for the group.
5. Encourage questions about the product and test for comprehension.
6. Cross off the product in the catalog.

Leader: Check with Andrey and queue up the most recent improvement video that has been made.

Improvements
Leader calls on 6 people everyday about their current morning improvement.

Every day we focus on an improvement that has been made. Because everyone is required to make one 2 second improvement a day, it is easy to showcase and celebrate one improvement every day. We take the improvements that are the most compelling and actually produce short videos showing the problem and improvement. These videos are then posted on our website under Lean Improvements.

The concept of reviewing an improvement every day comes from the idea that if you want to make a culture stick you must do the following 3 things:

- Create an expectation: Our expectation is that everyone makes a 2 second improvement everyday.

- Inspect the expectation: This is done in the first hour of every day during the Morning Improvement walk where we inspect the improvements that every team member is making.

- Reinforce the expectation: This is done by showing everyone videos of the improvements being made on a daily basis. Note: in the beginning we reviewed improvements by walking from department to department. This method may be effective for smaller companies, however as we grew it was more effective to make videos of the improvements and show them in the morning meeting.

2 Second Lean™

QR Code Link
(PDF format)
http://bit.ly/xNSQoa

Leader: Read one principle and discuss with group the meaning and how to apply it at work and home.

FastCap's 20 Principles

1) What is the purpose of FastCap? **Grow People.**
2) FastCap is always looking for a way to make things... **Faster, Safer and Simpler.**
3) Winston Churchill said these words... **"Action This Day".**
4) When we walk away from something we... **"Leave It Better Than You Found It".**
5) Our job title is ... **Process Engineer.**
6) Everything of value comes after... **Much hard work.**
7) Our goal each day is to make one... **Two second improvement.**
8) The most powerful word in the human language is... **A Person's Name.**
9) Enjoy your day to the fullest by... **Doing the Hard thing First.**
10) If we want to know what the real issue is, we must... **Ask why 5 times.**
11) When there is a problem, we should always... **Go and See.**
12) What must we do if we want to understand our actions... **Hansei** (reflect).
13) Real learning comes when you ask... **Questions.**
14) What did Bob Taylor say? **Responsible for things and people.**
15) "I'll trade all the intelligence in the world for someone with vision".
16) Toyota never attempts to improve anything unless they can... **Cut the waste in half.**
17) Hold each other accountable.
18) Your success at FastCap will be determined by the fact that you are... **Never Satisfied.**
19) Toyota's success is the result of the relentless pursuit of ... **Building a Culture.**
20) How do you make a vision stick?

Leader: Queue up and review the video, audio or book that provides our History and Personal Improvement lesson for the day.

History

Examples:
America the Story of Us video.
Top 100 people of the Century video.
Today in History

Personal Growth/Enrichment

Examples:
Read one page from book or listen to 5 minutes audiobook.
Good to Great
The Toyota Way
Nido Qubein

Leader: Ask one team member about one amendment per day.

Constitution

1st Amendment (1791, George Washington):
Freedom of Religion, Speech, Press, Assembly & Petition.

2nd Amendment (1791, George Washington):
A well regulated Militia Right to Keep and Bear Arms.

3rd Amendment (1791, George Washington):
No Soldier shall be quartered without consent.

4th Amendment (1791, George Washington):
Right to be secure
No unreasonable search and seizure
No warrants without probable cause, sworn by oath
Particularly describing place to be searched, persons or things to be seized

5th Amendment (1791, George Washington):
No person shall be held to answer for Capital or Infamous
Crime without indictment by Grand Jury, Except Military
No Double Jeopardy of life or limb
Shall not be compelled to bear witness against oneself
Shall not be deprived of Life, Liberty, or Property without due process of law

6th Amendment (1791, George Washington):
Right to a speedy trial by a jury of their peers
Be informed of the accusation against them
Confront witnesses against them
Compulsory process of witnesses in their favor
Assistance of Counsel for defense

7th Amendment (1791, George Washington):
Suits of common law exceeding 20 dollars, right to trial by jury
No fact shall be re-examined, other than by rules of common law

8th Amendment (1791, George Washington):
Excessive bail shall not be set
Nor excessive fines imposed
Nor Cruel and Unusual punishment inflicted

Leader: Lead team in a 3-5 minute stretch for the day.

Stretching

Grow People

- Take LEAN home
- Attitude of Gratitude, kindness to other workers
- Learning every day (History, Culture, Literature, Constitution)
- Hold each other accountable

Goals
Sample Pages

http://bit.ly/xMn1R4

Poka-Yoke

- Mistake-proof every process
- Create a simple process that anyone can follow in 5 minutes of training
- Less than one mistake a week
- Make things simple so we can free up RAM memory for higher-level thinking

One 2 Second Improvement

- Everyone makes One 2 Second Improvement every day for the rest of their life.
- Make the goal so small that anyone can achieve it.

No Bleeding

- Zero accidents
- Zero missed days

Made in the U.S.A.

- Bring manufacturing home
- Make all products in U.S. within ten years. Start - 2007, Complete - 2017

Best in the World at Lean

- Weekly tours
- Disney ship mentality
- Leave it better than you found it
- Morning meeting, build a culture
- Morning improvement from 7-8 am
- Video of improvements to help others
- Make one 2 Second Improvement a day

Same-Day Shipping

- Fax to truck in 2 hours

Raving Fans

- If customers don't rave, we've failed
- Use person's name 2x's in 1st minute
- Attitude of gratitude, blow them away
- 1 minute product video on all products
- Create a binder of Raving Fan letters

No Assuming No Guessing

- Ask why
- Ask why
- Ask why
- Make sure you are 1000% before you proceed.

World Class Problem Solvers

- Give me a solution
- No Excuses!! Don't tell me why you can't do it!
- History tells us that many others have overcome much bigger obstacles than we will ever face.

Improve the life of our Customer

- 100% Focus
- Zero waste of time
- Improve quality
- Reduce costs
- Don't make the customer pay for misuse of time and resources

Easy 8 Step Process
Sample Pages

KIDS CAN CLEAN THE KITCHEN & DO DISHES

1 — Scrub and rinse off stuck food	**2** — Place dishes in dishwasher from right to left; Sort silverware into slots for easy removal
3 — Sort glasses: Tall stuff on the sides, short stuff in the middle; Tupperware on top rack	**4** — Put dishwasher detergent in well
5 — Normal Wash; Start	**6** — Bleach water on counters & stove; Wipe down face of dishwasher; Use counter sponge to wipe down
7 — Clean sink strainer	**8** — Wipe down sink with bleach water

Download Word Template from our Lean Webpage

http://bit.ly/xNSQoa

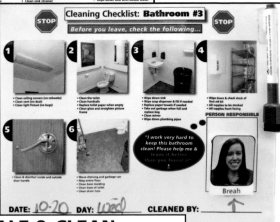

STOP Cleaning Checklist: **Bathroom #3** **STOP**

Before you leave, check the following...

1 — Clean ceiling corners (no cobwebs); Clean vent (no dust); Clean light fixture (no bugs)	**2** — Clean the toilet; Clean handrails; Replace toilet paper when empty; Clean glass and straighten picture frame
3 — Wipe down sink; Replace soap dispenser & fill if needed; Replace paper towels if needed; Take out garbage when full and replace bag; Clean mirror; Wipe down plumbing pipes	**4** — Wipe down & check stock of first aid kit; All supplies to be stocked; All supplies front facing — **PERSON RESPONSIBLE**
5 — Clean & disinfect inside and outside door handle	**6** — Move shelving and garbage can; Mop entire floor; Clean base-molding; Clean base of toilet; Clean drain hole

"I work very hard to keep this bathroom clean! Please help me & leave it better than you found it"

Breah

DATE: 10-20 **DAY:** Wed **CLEANED BY:** _____

DESCALE & CLEAN ESPRESSO MACHINE

1 — Fill reservoir with water and pour in one packet of Descaler & Cleaner; Find packets in bottom utensil drawer	**2** — Press MENU
3 — Press NEXT until you see DESCALE No	**4** — Press CHANGE; Choose YES to descale
5 — Press OK to confirm function	**6** — Place bowl under wand and spouts; Turn knob to start cycle; Empty bowl when cycle is over
7 — Rinse out reservoir of all descaler and cleaner; Fill with water; Repeat descaling process (Step 2-6)	**8** — Clean and dry bowl; Put away

Biography of Paul Akers

Paul Akers is founder and president of FastCap LLC, based in Bellingham, WA. FastCap is an international product development company founded in 1997 with over 2000 distributors worldwide. A prolific inventor, Paul holds US and international patents. His company, FastCap, launches approximately 20 new innovative products per year and has won business of the year in 1999 and 2010. Paul and his wife, Leanne, have built FastCap from their garage into a multi-million dollar company in 13 years.

As an instrument rated pilot, Paul flies his own corporate aircraft conducting business in over 40 countries. He has over 2000 hours of flight time, which includes 3 North Atlantic crossings.

Paul is a master craftsman, gardener and designer. He built his own exquisite Greene and Greene craftsman style home in Bellingham, Washington, as well as the furniture and guitars in his home.

Paul's grandparents emigrated from Greece in 1913 through Ellis Island. Nicholas and Amelia taught him to appreciate the gift of America and the boundless opportunities it provides to millions of people from around the world.

Paul was born and raised in Southern California, and was drawn towards excellence and high standards from an early age. He earned his Eagle Scout at age 14. Inspired by woodworking artisans he earned awards and recognition for furniture design before graduating high school. At the age of 15 he built his own guitar and earned the attention of guitar designer Bob Taylor, who mentored and eventually put Paul to work for Taylor Guitars. As a true American innovator, Bob made a lasting impression on Paul, where he was part of building over 2000 world class musical instruments.

He graduated from Biola University in 1983 with honors, obtaining a degree in education with an emphasis in Greek and German.

Paul and Leanne started from humble beginnings. They bought their first home, an abandoned gang house in La Puente, California. "Complete every project before starting a new one," was Paul's mantra, and this attitude afforded him many amazing opportunities.

Paul worked in Pasadena restoring some of the most prestigious historical homes and became part of an exclusive group of craftsmen that built the home for the editor of Architectural Digest. Paul taught Industrial Arts at Mark Keppel High school where his innovative thinking led to the development of a program that focused on teaching kids to actually build furniture, rather than the standard high school projects like key racks and cutting boards.

Paul also served as a pastor at Glassell Park Baptist Church in the inner city of Los Angeles.

He catapulted into the business world when his knack for problem solving led to an invention, and eventually his own manufacturing business that started in his garage. Through a series of twists and turns he discovered Lean and the Toyota Production System (TPS) which helped to launch his business from the garage into the successful international product development company known as Fastcap.

Using Lean, Paul's company has prospered and expanded even in the current economic downturn. He has never laid off one employee, nor cut one salary and currently offers the highest entry level pay for any business in the region.

Paul is an avid outdoorsman and has 3 times summited Mt. Whitney at 14,495 feet, the highest peak in the continental US.

Paul is an energetic speaker whose core passion is helping people discover their full potential in life and teaching others how to implement Lean thinking for their own business and personal success.

His weekly radio show "The American Innovator" is listened to by thousands every Saturday morning, where he teaches his listeners throughout North America the power of innovation and lean thinking.

In 2010 Paul ran for the US Senate in Washington State on a lean platform of transforming government by empowering people. After the election Paul launched Lean America, to donate his time teaching Lean thinking and creating a lean culture in government organizations throughout the country.

In June of 2011 Paul won the prestigious award of Business Executive of the year for Seattle Business Magazine.

Paul has been married for 28 years to his wife Leanne and has two children: Andréa and Kolbe.

In 2011 Paul wrote his first book about Lean Manufacturing, *2 Second Lean*.